ALSO BY ANTONIA FRASER

Mary Queen of Scots (1969)

Cromwell: The Lord Protector (1973)

King James VI and I (1975)

The Lives of the Kings and Queens of England (editor) (1975)

LOVE LETTERS

An Anthology

LOVE LETTERS

An Anthology Chosen by

ANTONIA FRASER

Alfred A. Knopf

NEW YORK

1977

THIS IS A BORZOI BOOK
PUBLISHED BY ALFRED A. KNOPF, INC.

Copyright © 1976, 1977 by Antonia Fraser

Since this page cannot legibly accommodate all acknowledgements,
they appear on pages xii–xvi.

Library of Congress Cataloging in Publication Data
Main entry under title:
Love letters.
Bibliography: p.
1. Love-letters. I. Fraser, Lady Antonia Pakenham, [date]
PN6140.L7L57   1977   808.86′9′354   76–47924
ISBN 0–394–41278–8

Manufactured in the United States of America

First American Edition

for Harold

Contents

[vii]

FEARS AND WORRIES

ECSTASIES

PASSIONS

JEALOUSIES

GALLANTRIES

SEPARATIONS

FAREWELLS

UNIONS

NATURE OF LOVE

TOTAL LOVE

ABOUT LETTERS

Acknowledgements

AUTHOR'S NOTE

In choosing the letters for this anthology, I owe a great deal to two people in particular. First, to Judith Burnley, whose idea it was. Second, to Patricia Hale, whose industrious and imaginative research made the whole project possible: my debt to her is literally inestimable. Beyond that I wish to thank my former secretary Angela Cock, Hilary Arnold of Weidenfeld and Nicolson and two distinguished scholars – Ivan Morris (who died tragically while this book was going to press) and Michael Grant – for advice on their respective Ancient Worlds. Beyond that, there were a host of friends, led as ever by George Marek . . . I trust they will accept the inclusion of their candidate in this book as the grateful acknowledgement it is intended to be.

BIOGRAPHICAL NOTES

The Biographical Details and further reading were researched and compiled by Rosemary Canter.

TRANSLATORS

The letter from Chopin (pages 158–60) was translated from the Polish by George Marek. The letter from Lady Shigenari (page 163) was translated from the Japanese by Ivan Morris. The letter from Lucrezia Borgia (page 147) was translated from the Italian by Paul Gronau. The following letters were translated from the French by Christine Czechowski: from Stendahl (pages 22 and 194); from Liszt (pages 66–7 and 218); from Balzac (pages 69–70); from Napoleon (pages 79, 79–81, 191–2 and 217); from Juliette Drouet (page 81); from Proust (page 148); from Victor Hugo (pages 149–52); from Baudelaire (page

213); from Marie d'Agoult (page 218); from the Prince de Joinville (page 219).

* *

Grateful acknowledgement is made to the following for permission to reprint previously published and copyrighted letters.

George Allen & Unwin Ltd.: The letters from John Ruskin (pages 92–3) and from Effie Gray (page 93). Reprinted from *The Order of Release* by John Ruskin. Courtesy of the publisher.

Brandt & Brandt: The letter from Dorothy Thompson (pages 183–4). Reprinted from *Sinclair Lewis: An American Life* by Mark Schorer. Copyright © 1961 by Mark Schorer. Published by McGraw-Hill Book Company. Reprinted by permission of the author's agent.

Curtis Brown Ltd.: The letter from Pierre Curie (pages 8–9). Reprinted from *Madame Curie* by Eve Curie. Copyright 1937 by Doubleday and Co., Inc. Reprinted by permission of the author's agent.

Cassell and Company Ltd.: The letter from Marie Bashkirtseff (pages 16–17). Reprinted from *The Letters of Marie Bashkirtseff*, translated by Mary J. Serrano (1891). Courtesy of the publisher.

J. M. Dent and Sons Ltd.: The letter from Robert Burns (pages 10–12). Reprinted from *The Love Songs and Heroines of Robert Burns*.

E. P. Dutton and Co., Inc.: The letter of the Fair Maid of Astolat (pages 40–1). Reprinted from *Le Morte d'Arthur* by Sir Thomas Malory. An Everyman's Library Edition. . . . The letters from Margery Brews (pages 3–4 and 50–1). Reprinted from *The Paston Letters,* edited, with an introduction by John Warrington. An Everyman's Library Edition. . . . The letters from Dorothy Osborne (pages 55–7, 154–5 and 193). Reprinted from *Letters to Sir William Temple* by Dorothy Osborne, edited and annotated by Edward A. Parry. An Everyman's Library Edition.

Granada Publishing Ltd.: The letters from Henrik Ibsen (page 53) and from Emile Bardach (pages 53–4). Reprinted from Michael Meyer's biography of Ibsen, Volume III.

Harcourt Brace Jovanovich, Inc.: The letter from Oscar Wilde (pages 63–4). Reprinted from *Letters of Oscar Wilde,* edited by Rupert Hart-Davis. Copyright © 1962 by Vyvyan Holland.

Harper & Row Publishers, Inc.: The letter from Anton Chekov (pages 139–41). Reprinted from *Letters of Anton Chekov,* selected by Simon Karlinsky, translated from the Russian by Michael Henry Heim.

Introduction

As a love letter is – or should be – the most personal form of document most of us write, this is a highly personal anthology. I chose the letters in it for reasons of personal predilection, and following my fancy, I have gone for the heart on the sleeve, or at any rate on paper, the heart that shows. This is not therefore a peculiarly literary collection, still less a scholarly one. Favourites chose themselves, but not according to the rules of literature: John Keats did prove himself, as I had always believed since girlhood, to have written the greatest love letters in the English language, but two other favourites were Zelda Fitzgerald and Dorothy Osborne, in their own very different ways great lovers rather than great artists. I eliminated boldly some famous names – including George Bernard Shaw – whose letters aroused in me the suspicion that they were written for effect, the sweet accents of style rather than the raw voice of love.

Some of these letters inevitably arouse the question: what happened next? Did the writer live happily – or pine unrequitedly – ever after? The short answer might be: Disraeli – the former, despite his superb, proud letter of self-justification following his apparent rejection by Mary Anne. Mary Wollstonecraft – the latter, in spite of her wonderful, poignant realization in a letter to Gilbert Imlay that in the face of their child lay the true meaning of the union of a man and woman as one flesh. Michael Faraday went on to enjoy an exceptionally happy marriage to Sarah Barnard, for all his hesitations; Victor Hugo on the other hand rivalled and somewhat resembled Jove as a womanizer, for all his protestations to Adèle. Mrs Kailash Puri, who as a schoolgirl received the letter from her future husband about to proceed to Lucknow University – 'Won't you darling write me an essay on love?' – has lived in great fulfilment ever since. To satisfy this natural curiosity, brief biographical details will be found at the back of the book. But in general this is not intended to be a volume of historical insights or textual criticisms* : although as a former student of Oliver Cromwell myself, I was delighted and amused to discover that Thomas Carlyle, whether consciously or not, had borrowed a phrase – 'thou art dearer to me than any creature' – from one of Oliver's letters to his wife when Carlyle wrote to Jane, shortly after he had finished his own work on the subject.

It is for the emotion, or state of love expressed therein, that these letters are chosen. They are therefore divided into emotional categories rather than arranged in chronological, alphabetical or geographical order. I certainly cannot claim this to be an all-inclusive collection. There are many lost letters one would like to have glimpsed, including those engraved tablets of onyx and crystal which Cleopatra used to send to Antony, according to Plutarch, while he was administering justice in the tribunal. Alas, for all their durable material, these love letters have quite vanished, and Plutarch's description serves merely to tantalise. Then there are those who, like the protagonist of W. H. Auden's poem 'Who's Who' (he 'answered some of his long marvellous letters but kept none'), have preferred the eternal reticence of destruction. And I dare say that there are many letters whose very passion condemned them to the furnace, even if it did not exactly burn the paper they were written on; in which connection, it is interesting to note that Chopin's letter to Delphine Potocka has not been published in its full unbowdlerized form before. If genuine – and it must be admitted that grave scholarly doubts have been raised on the subject – then as a discussion of the possible wastage of the artist's efforts in the act of love

---

*Thus, in most cases, the letters reproduce the spellings and punctuation of the originals.

(not the line, incidentally, that Burns took) it is surely unique in its frankness.

Certain other aspects of a love letter are inevitably lost in a collection of this sort. How important is the actual physical appearance of a letter! A thousand years ago at the court of the Japanese Emperor, no gentleman would have dreamt of spending a night with a lady without sending round a letter of appreciation the morning after – a letter in which the thickness, size, design and colour of the paper all helped to indicate the emotional mood that the writer wished to suggest, the finishing touch being supplied by the branch or spray of blossom which it was *de rigueur* to attach to it. Such urgent scrutiny of a letter for clues is not unknown to lovers in our own western civilisation, even if the rules are less clear cut. Edith Wharton summed up the crucial moment of arrival: 'the first glance to see how many pages there are, the second to see how it ends, the breathless first reading, the slow lingering over each phrase and each word, the taking possession, the absorbing of them, one by one, and finally the choosing of the one that will be carried in one's thoughts all day, making an exquisite accompaniment to the dull prose of life'. While that moment of rapture can scarcely be imprisoned within the confines of an anthology, I have tried at least to indicate the importance of it, by including a few beginnings and endings to love letters that have taken my fancy – these being so often the gates of heaven (or hell) for expectant lovers.

As to definition of a love letter, there are no rules in this collection except my own reactions to the subject. I suppose the love of a woman for a man or vice versa constitutes the predominant emotion (although I have made no attempt to reckon which, if either, sex predominates as the actual writer). But there is also the plea of Theon, the schoolboy whose father has left him behind, which from the second century speaks to us as strongly of love as Carrington's searing letter to Lytton Strachey in the twentieth. Sir Thomas More's great farewell letter was written to his daughter Margaret Roper, not his wife. Ida John's unforgettable expostulation of jealousy was written to Dorelia, the Other Woman, not to her husband, Augustus. A more enlightened generation than Oscar Wilde's can see that his letter to Lord Alfred Douglas (quoted at Wilde's trial) is about love indeed . . .

It will be remarked that three entries are fictional in origin, and it may be asked, if any are to be included, why only three? In fact, I have made no effort to comb literature: everyone will have their own nominees in this respect, and indeed during my researches my friends were not slow to suggest the great love letters of fiction, whereas I should have much preferred them to turn out their own. It's just that of the three entries, two do not seem to me to be fictional at all, so impressed am I by the vehemence of their emotion. I last read of Roddy's terrible rebuff of Judy in Rosamond Lehmann's *Dusty Answer* when I was the same age as the heroine; I thought I should never forget it, and indeed when I went back to check the passage for inclusion in this book, I found that I was right: I actually did remember it word for word. The same applies to a more recently suffered rejection, that of Anna in Jean Rhys's *Voyage in the Dark*. As for the story of the death of the Fair Maid of Astolat – that is the most beautiful physical image of a letter I know, clasped in the white hand of the girl as she floats down the river in her black-decked barget.

It is not only concerning fiction that people's reactions to love letters vary singularly. Lucrezia Borgia's letter to Cardinal Bembo is included here because Byron thought this correspondence (studied in a library in Milan) the most beautiful he had ever read: 'very simple, sweet and to the purpose'. Perhaps he was partly brought to that conviction by the lock of Lucrezia's hair he found with the letters – 'the prettiest and fairest imaginable'; once again the physical is hard to reproduce. As against that, it is touching, if slightly pathetic, to record the complacent reaction of Frances Stevenson, Lloyd George's mistress, to the letters of Heloise and Abelard: 'He was a world-renowned philosopher and logician and she was just a beautiful and intelligent girl. All sorts of misfortunes overtake them, and they end their days in a monastery and a convent respectively. They did not manage things very well', ends the practical Miss Stevenson. 'And I think I know two people who would have arranged things better.'

In principle, in my search after the heart, I have made no attempt to pursue any letters where the lovers have gained prominence because of their political connections – neither Miss Stevenson herself, Asquith to Venetia Montagu, nor the recently emerged letters of Sir John French are featured here, since such material seems to me of more interest to the historian or biographer than the anthologist. The letter of the International Socialist Rosa Luxemburg to her comrade Leo Jogiches is on the other hand an epistle of pure love. It begins with this classic thank-you for a gift – to those used to rather different *gages d'amour* such as turtle doves or even jewels – 'You simply cannot imagine how pleased I am with your choice. Why, Rodbertus is simply my favourite economist and I can read him a hundred times for sheer intellectual pleasure'. That opening only serves to contrast with the change of tone and the pathetic plea for 'our own little room, our own furniture, a library of our own, quiet and regular work . . . And perhaps even a little, a very little, baby?'

The categories themselves formed their own pattern, suggested to me by the letters rather than the reverse. DECLARATIONS, starting with young Margery Brews of the fifteenth-century Paston letters, runs through to PLEAS and to REJECTIONS, and thus naturally to FEARS AND WORRIES, including Joyce's tortured letter to Nora Barnacle before their union (which should have warned her . . .). Then ECSTASIES, the white side of love, with Sophia Peabody's lovely salute to the year in which she first met her future husband Nathaniel Hawthorne, written on December 31st: 'God bless you this night of the old year. It has proved the year of our nativity. Has not the old earth passed away from us? – are not all things new?' PASSIONS – the white and the black sides of love – finds Byron represented in both colours, to Caroline Lamb and Teresa Guiccioli. This category begins with Keats, and Napoleon follows him close (and indeed Napoleon proved himself one of the most irresistible of torrid letter-writers when it came to the process of selection). JEALOUSIES, in contrast, is black.

SEPARATIONS, it is scarcely necessary to observe, showed itself a rich category: but the circumstances of separation differed widely, from Charles Stewart Parnell in Kilmainham Gaol writing to Katharine O'Shea, to Chekhov away from his actress wife Olga, to Bert Fielder the ordinary soldier at the front in the 1914 war, to Alexander Hamilton in the American War of Independence, whose letter to his wife shows the same concept of love and honour as Lovelace to Lucasta in a very different contest.

FAREWELLS, like UNIONS, turned out to be weighted in favour of marriage, with Catherine of Aragon's last message to Henry VIII providing a bitter counterpoint to his urgent amorous letter to Anne Boleyn. In the category TOTAL LOVE, I have tried to re-create the extraordinary all-absorbing intensity of certain passions, which can bring ruin as easily as reward, from a sixteenth-century love letter translated from the Japanese in which the young wife of Kimura Shigenari tells her husband she intends to kill herself before he dies in battle, to Dorothy Thompson's moving letter to Sinclair Lewis refusing him a divorce. In ABOUT LETTERS, Kafka expresses in its most extreme form, as he expresses most things, the feeling we have all had at one time or another, that it might be better to be sure of a letter *not* coming rather than expect one which does not arrive. IN BRIEF is a final salute to the genre, and hints at another common anxiety – the suspicion that at the end of writing that long, long letter, the letter that says it all, it might have been better simply to inscribe the three words: 'I love you'.

It will be obvious from all this that I am on the side of love letters. I do not, for example, share the view of Aldous Huxley's that they are in the main commonplace (the anonymous suicide note quoted here, which he found in a newspaper, was in his view the exception that proved the rule). It seems to me that Rousseau made a much better point in the Introduction to *La*

Nouvelle Héloïse, when he observed that 'in real love-letters, the thoughts are common, yet the style is not familiar'. There is also the fact that anyone can write a love letter and almost everybody has: one should beware of those who boast of never having fallen in love – there is either something missing somewhere or else the boaster is subtly begging to be roused from his or her frozen state of inanition.

Nor do I believe that the love letter itself is dead, as opposed to the love call on the telephone, for the simple human reason that letters can be carried around as talismans to refresh the memory, while love calls can merely be recollected in tranquillity and the memory may not refresh them. With all due respect to Marshall McLuhan, it is the transportability of the written or printed word which will always be its saving. John Ruskin told Effie Gray in the happier days of their relationship that he would soon know her letters by heart: nevertheless he would have liked to have them printed, in a little pocket volume, to carry about with him always. It is to be hoped that the present volume will serve as a printed present for lovers whose own letters are in short supply, or have fallen to bits from wear and tear. Who knows, some of the letters may even serve as models for the laggard or the unimaginative. It is best, however, to choose one of the obscurer entries for total plagiarism: my father, reciting 'Now sleeps the crimson petal, now the white' when courting my mother, and then adding solemnly: 'I wrote that', was felt to have gone rather far in his assumption of her ignorance of English literature. Nevertheless the principle was a good one. It is certainly possible to be more patently persistent through the medium of a barrage of love letters than any other form. As Ovid pointed out to young men in *The Art of Love:* 'In time refractory oxen come to plough, in time horses are taught to bear the pliant reins, an iron ring is worn by constant use, a curved share wastes by constant ploughing of the ground . . . Only persevere, you will overcome Penelope herself'. Two thousand years later Ovid's advice still holds good.

Lastly, lest this anthology seem to have become a sort of *vade mecum* for aspiring lovers – whereas its primary purpose is to give delight to all comers, the loved and unloved, the loving and the stony-hearted – let us remember the wise observation of Lord Byron on the subject of old letters: one of the pleasures of reading them is the knowledge that they need no answer. None of the letters in this anthology needs an answer – although some of them may provoke an inspiration.

– ANTONIA FRASER

DECLARATIONS

MARGERY BREWS to SIR JOHN PASTON

[February 1477]

To my right well-beloved cousin, John Paston,
Esquire, be this letter delivered, etc.

Right worshipful and well-beloved Valentine, in my most
humble wise I recommend me unto you, etc. And heartily I thank
you for the letter which that ye sent me by John Bickerton,
whereby I understand and know that ye be purposed to come to
Topcroft in short time, and without any errand or matter but only
to have a conclusion of the matter betwixt my father and you. I
would be most glad of any creature alive, so that the matter might
grow to effect. And thereas ye say, an' ye come and find the matter
no more towards you than ye did aforetime, ye would no more put
my father and my lady my mother to no cost nor business for that
cause a good while after; which causeth mine heart to be full
heavy. And if that ye come, and the matter take to none effect,
then should I be much more sorry and full of heaviness.

And as for myself, I have done and understood in the matter
that I can or may, as God knoweth; and I let you plainly
understand that my father will no more money part withal in that
behalf, but £100 and 50 marks, which is right far from the
accomplishment of your desire.

Wherefore, if that ye could be content with that good and my
poor person, I would be the merriest maiden on ground. And if ye
think not yourself so satisfied, or that ye might have much more
good (as I have understood by you afore) – good, true, and loving
Valentine, that ye take no such labour upon you as to come more
for that matter, but let it pass, and never more to be spoken of, as I

[3]

may be your true lover and beadswoman during my life.

No more unto you at this time, but Almighty Jesus preserve you both body and soul, etc.

By your Valentine,
Margery Brews

BENJAMIN DISRAELI to MARY ANNE WYNDHAM LEWIS

[Park Street. Thursday night, 7 February, 1839]
I wd have endeavoured to have spoken to you of that which it was necessary you shd know, & I wished to have spoken with the calmness which was natural to one humiliated & distressed. I succeeded so far as to be considered a 'selfish bully' & to be desired to quit your house for ever. I have recourse therefore to this miserable method of communicating with you; none can be more imperfect but I write as if it were the night before my execution.

Every hour of my life I hear of an approaching union from all lips except your own. At last a friend anxious to distinguish me by some unusual mark of his favor & thinking to confer on me a distinction of which I shd be proud, offers me one of his seats for our happy month. The affair was then approaching absurdity. There was a period, & a much earlier one, when similar allusions to the future & intimations of what must occur were frequent from your lips; as if you thought some daily hint of the impending result was necessary to stimulate or to secure my affection.

As a woman of the world, which you are thoroughly, you ought not, you cannot be, unacquainted with the difference that subsists between our relative positions. The continuance of the present state of affairs cd only render you disreputable; me it wd render infamous. There is only one construction which Society, & justly, puts upon a connection between a woman who is supposed to be rich & a man whom she avowedly loves & does not marry. In

[4]

England especially there is no stigma more damning; it is one which no subsequent conduct or position ever permits to be forgotten. It has crushed men who have committed with impunity even crimes; some things may indeed be more injurious; none more ignominious.

This reputation impends over me. I will at least preserve that honor which is the breath of my existence. At present I am in the position of an insolvent whose credit is not suspected; but ere a few weeks I must inevitably chuse between being ridiculous or being contemptible; I must be recognised as being jilted, or I must at once sink into what your friend Lady Morgan has already styled me 'Mrs. Wyndham Lewis's De Novo.'

This leads me to the most delicat of subjects, but in justice to us both I will write with the utmost candor. I avow, when I first made my advances to you I was influenced by no romantic feelings. My father had long wished me to marry; my settling in life was the implied tho' not stipulated, condition of a disposition of his property, which wd have been convenient to me. I myself, about to commence a practical career, wished for the solace of a home, & shrunk from all the torturing passions of intrigue. I was not blind to worldly advantages in such an alliance, but I had already proved that my heart was not to be purchased. I found you in sorrow, & that heart was touched. I found you, as I thought, aimiable, tender, & yet acute & gifted with no ordinary mind – one whom I cd look upon with pride as the partner of my life, who cd sympathise with all my projects & feelings, console me in the moments of depression, share my hour of triumph, & work with me for our honor & happiness.

Now for your fortune: I write the sheer truth. That fortune proved to be much less than I, or the world, imagined. It was in fact, as far as I was concerned, a fortune which cd not benefit me in the slightest degree; it was merely a jointure not greater than your station required; enough to maintain your establishment & gratify your private tastes. To eat & to sleep in that house & nominally to call it mine – these cd be only objects for a penniless adventurer. Was this an inducement for me to sacrifice my sweet liberty, & that indefinite future wh: is one of the charms of existence? No, when months ago I told you there was only one link between us, I felt that my heart was inextricably engaged to you, & but for that I wd have terminated our acquaintance. From that moment I devoted to you all the passion of my being. Alas! It has been poured upon the sand.

As time progressed I perceived in your character & in mine own certain qualities, wh: convinced me that if I wished to persevere that profound & unpolluted affection wh: subsisted between us money must never be introduced. Had we married, not one shilling of your income shd ever have been seen by me; neither indirectly nor directly, wd I have interfered in the management of your affairs. If Society justly stigmatizes with infamy the hired lover, I shrink with equal disgust from being the paid husband.

You have branded me as selfish – Alas! I fear you have apparent cause. I confess it with the most heart rending humiliation. Little did I think when I wept, when in a manner so unexpected & so irresistible you poured upon my bosom the treasured savings of your affection, that I received the wages of my degradation! Weak, wretched fool! This led to my accepting your assistance in my trial; but that was stipulated to be a loan & I only waited for the bill which my agent gave me when you were at Bradenham as the balance of our accounts & which becomes due this very month, to repay it into yr bankers.

By heavens as far as worldly interests are concerned, your aliance cd not benefit me. All that society can offer is at my command; it is not the apparent possession of a jointure that ever elevates position. I can live, as I live, without disgrace, until the inevitable progress of events gives me that independence which is all I require. I have entered into these ungracious details because you reproached me with my interested views. No; I wd not condescend to be the minion of a princess; and not all the gold of Ophir shd ever lead me to the altar. Far different are the qualities which I require in the sweet participator of my existence. My nature demands that my life shall be perpetual love.

Upon your general conduct to me I make no comment. It is now useless. I will not upbraid you. I will only blame myself. All warned me: public and private – all were eager to save me from the perdition into which I have fallen. Coxcomb to suppose that you wd conduct yourself to me in a manner different to that in which you have behaved to fifty others!

And yet I thought I had touched your heart! Wretched Idiot!

As a woman of the world you must have foreseen this. And for the gratification of your vanity, for the amusement of ten months, for the diversion of your seclusion, could you find the heart to do this? Was there no ignoble prey at hand that you must degrade a bird of heaven? Why not have let your Captain Neil have been the minion of your gamesome hours with humiliating & debasing me. Nature never intended me for a toy & dupe. But you have struck deep. You have done that which my enemies have yet failed to do: you have broken my spirit. From the highest to the humblest scene of my life, from the brilliant world of fame to my own domestic hearth, you have poisoned all. I have no place of refuge: home is odious, the world oppressive.

Triumph – I seek not to conceal my state. It is not sorrow, it is not wretchedness; it is anguish, it is the *endurance* of that pang which is the passing characteristic of agony. All that can prostrate a man has fallen on my victim head. My heart outraged, my pride wounded, my honor nearly tainted. I know well that ere a few days can pass I shall be the scoff & jest of that world, to gain whose admiration has been the effort of my life. I have only one source of solace – the consciousness of self-respect. Will that uphold me? A terrible problem that must quickly be solved.

Farewell. I will not affect to wish you happiness for it is not in your nature to obtain it. For a few years you may flutter in some frivolous circle. But the time will come when you will sigh for any heart that could be fond and despair of one that can be faithful. Then will be the penal hour of retribution; then you will recall to your memory the passionate heart that you have forfeited, and the genius you have betrayed.

D

PIERRE CURIE to MARIE SKLODOVSKA

[10 August, 1894]

Nothing could have given me greater pleasure than to get news of you. The prospect of remaining two months without hearing about you had been extremely disagreeable to me: that is to say, your little note was more than welcome.

I hope you are laying up a stock of good air and that you will come back to us in October. As for me, I think I shall not go anywhere; I shall stay in the country, where I spend the whole day in front of my open window or in the garden.

We have promised each other – haven't we? – to be at least great friends. If you will only not change your mind! For there are no promises that are binding; such things cannot be ordered at will. It would be a fine thing, just the same, in which I hardly dare believe, to pass our lives near each other, hypnotized by our dreams: *your* patriotic dreams, *our* humanitarian dream, and *our* scientific dream.

Of all those dreams the last is, I believe, the only legitimate one. I mean by that we are powerless to change the social order and, even if we were not, we should not know what to do; in taking action, no matter in what direction, we should never be sure of not doing more harm than good, by retarding some inevitable evolution. From the scientific point of view, on the contrary, we may hope to do something; the ground is solider here, and any discovery that we may make, however small, will remain acquired knowledge.

See how it works out: it is agreed that we shall be great friends, but if you leave France in a year it would be an altogether too Platonic friendship, that of two creatures who would never see each other again. Wouldn't it be better for you to stay with me? I know that this question angers you, and that you don't want to speak of it again – and then, too, I feel so thoroughly unworthy of you from every point of view.

I thought of asking your permission to meet you *by chance* in Fribourg. But you are staying there, unless I am mistaken, only one day, and on that day you will of course belong to our friends the Kovalskis.

Believe me your very devoted

Pierre Curie

I should be happy if you would write to me and give me the assurance that you intend to come back in October. If you write direct to Sceaux the letters would get to me quicker: Pierre Curie, 13 rue des Sablons, Sceaux (Seine).

ALFRED DE MUSSET to GEORGE SAND

[1833]

My dear George,

I have something stupid [*bête*] and ridiculous to tell you. I am foolishly writing you instead of having told you this, I do not know why, when returning from that walk. To-night I shall be annoyed at having done so. You will laugh in my face, will take me for a maker of phrases in all my relations with you hitherto. You will show me the door and you will think I am lying. I am in love with you. I have been thus since the first day I called on you. I thought I should cure myself in seeing you quite simply as a friend. There are many things in your character which could cure me; I have tried to convince myself of that as much as I could. But I pay too dearly for the moments I pass with you. I prefer to tell you and I have done well, because I shall suffer much less if I am cured by your showing me the door now. This night during which . . .* I had decided to let you know that I was out of town, but I do not want to make a mystery of it nor have the appearance of quarrelling without a reason. Now George, you will say: 'Another fellow, who is about to become a nuisance,' as you say. If I am not quite the firstcomer for you, tell me, as you would have

---

* George Sand, who edited this letter herself for publication, deleted a small section here.

told me yesterday in speaking of somebody else, what I ought to do. But I beg of you, if you intend to say that you doubt the truth of what I am writing, then I had rather you did not answer me at all. I know how you think of me, and I have nothing to hope for in telling you this. I can only foresee losing a friend and the only agreeable hours I have passed for a month. But I know that you are kind, that you have loved, and I put my trust in you, not as a mistress, but as a frank and loyal comrade. George, I am an idiot to deprive myself of the pleasure of seeing you the short time you have still to spend in Paris, before your departure for Italy, where we would have spent such beautiful nights together, if I had the strength. But the truth is that I suffer, and that my strength is wanting.

Alfred de Musset

ROBERT BURNS to CLARINDA (AGNES MACLEHOSE)

Friday Evening,
21 December, 1787

I beg your pardon, my dear 'Clarinda', for the fragment scrawl I sent you yesterday. I really don't know what I wrote. A gentleman for whose character, abilities, and critical knowledge, I have the highest veneration, called in, just as I had begun the second sentence, and I would not make the Porter wait. I read to my much-respected friend several of my own bagatelles, and, among others, your lines, which I had copied out. He began some criticisms on them, as on the other pieces, when I informed him they were the work of a young lady in this town; which, I assure you, made him stare. My learned friend seriously protested, that he did not believe any young woman in Edinburgh was capable of such lines: and, if you know anything of Professor Gregory, you will neither doubt of his abilities nor his sincerity. I do love you, if possible, still better for having so fine a taste and turn for Poesy. I have again gone wrong in my usual unguarded way; but you may erase the word, and put esteem, respect, or any other tame Dutch expression you please in its place. I believe there is no holding converse, or carrying on correspondence with an amiable woman, much less a *gloriously-amiable, fine woman*, without some mixture of that delicious Passion, whose most devoted Slave I have, more than once, had the honour of being. But why be hurt or offended on that account? Can no honest man have a prepo[sse]ssion for a fine woman, but he must run his head against an intrigue? Take a little of the tender witchcraft of Love, and add it to the generous, the honourable sentiments of manly Friendship, and I know but *one* more delightful morsel, which few, few in any rank ever taste. Such a composition is like adding cream to strawberries: it not only gives the fruit a more elegant richness, but has a peculiar deliciousness of its own.

I enclose you a few lines I composed on a late melancholy occasion. I will not give about five or six copies of it at all; and I would be hurt if any friend should give any copies without my consent.

You cannot imagine, Clarinda (I like the idea of Arcadian names in a commerce of this kind), how much store I have set by the hopes of your future friendship. I don't know if you have a just idea of my character, but I wish you to see me *as I am*. I am, as most people of my trade are, a strange Will-o'-wisp being; the victim, too frequently, of much imprudence, and many follies. My great constituent elements are Pride and Passion: the first I have endeavoured to humanize into integrity and honour; the last makes me a Devotee, to the warmest degree of enthusiasm, in Love, Religion, or Friendship: either of them, or all together, as I happen to be inspired.

'Tis true I never saw you but once; but how much acquaintance did I form with you at that once! Do not think I flatter you, or have a design upon you, Clarinda: I have too much pride for the one, and too little cold contrivance for the other; but of all God's creatures I ever could approach in the beaten way of acquaintance, you struck me with the deepest, the strongest, the most permanent impression. I say the most permanent, because I know myself well, and how far I can promise either on my prepossessions or powers. Why are you unhappy? – and why are so many of our fellow-creatures, unworthy to belong to the same species with you, blest with all they can wish? You have a hand all-benevolent to give, – why were you denied the pleasure? You have a heart formed, gloriously formed, for all the most refined luxuries of love, – why was that heart ever wrung? O Clarinda! shall we not meet in a state, some yet unknown state of Being, where the lavish hand of Plenty shall minister to the highest wish of Benevolence, and where the chill north-wind of Prudence shall never blow over the flowery fields of Enjoyment? If we do not, Man was made in vain! I deserved most of the unhappy hours that have lingered over my head; they were the wages of my labour. But what unprovoked Demon, malignant as Hell, stole upon the confidence of unmistrusting, busy Fate, and dashed your cup of life with undeserved sorrow?

Let me know how long your stay will be out of town: I shall count the hours till you inform me of your return. Cursed etiquette forbids your seeing me just now; and so soon as I can walk I must bid Edinburgh adieu. Lord, why was I born to see misery which I cannot relieve, and to meet with friends whom I can't enjoy! I look back with the pang of unavailing avarice on my loss in not knowing you sooner.

All last winter, – these three months past, – what luxury of intercourse have I not lost! Perhaps, though, 'twas better for my peace. You see I am either above, or incapable of Dissimulation. I believe it is want of that particular genius. I despise Design, because I want either coolness or wisdom to be capable of it. – I may take a fort by storm, but never by Siege. I am interrupted.

Adieu, my dear Clarinda!

Sylvander

JUDY to RODDY in *Dusty Answer* by Rosamond Lehmann

She would write him a letter, tell him all; yes, she would tell him all. Her love for him need no longer be like a half-shameful secret. If she posted a letter to-night, he would get it to-morrow morning, just before he left.

She wrote:

> Roddy, this is to say good-bye once more and to send you all my love till we meet again. I do love you, indeed, in every sort of way, and to any degree you can possibly imagine; and beyond that more, more, more, unimaginably. The more my love for you annihilates me, the more it becomes a sense of inexhaustible power.
>
> Do you love me, Roddy? Tell me again that you do; and don't think me importunate.
>
> I am so wrapped round and rich in my thoughts of you that at the moment I feel I can endure your absence. I almost welcome it because it will give me time to sit alone, and begin to realise my happiness. So that when you come back – Oh Roddy, come back soon!
>
> I have loved you ever since I first saw you when we were little, I suppose, – only you, always you. I'm not likely ever to stop loving you. Thank God I can tell you so at last. Will you go on loving me? Am I to go on loving you? Oh but you won't say no, after last night. If you don't want to be tied quite yet, I shall understand. I can wait years quite happily, if you love me. Roddy I am yours. Last night I gave you what has always belonged to you. But I can't think about last night yet. It is too close and tremendous and shattering. I gasp and nearly faint when I try to recall it. I dissolve.
>
> When I came back to my room in the dawn I stared and stared at my face in the glass, wondering how it was I could recognize it. How is it I look the same, and move, eat, speak, much as usual?

[13]

Ought I to have been more coy, more reluctant last night? Would it have been more fitting – would you have respected me more? Was I too bold? Oh, this is foolishness: I had no will but yours. But because I love you so much I am a little fearful. So write to me quickly and tell me what to think, feel, do. I shall dream till then.

There is so much more to tell you, and yet it is all the same really. My darling, I love you!

Judy.

She posted it. Next morning she hurriedly dressed and ran downstairs in the sudden expectation of finding a letter from him; but there was none.

Now he would have got hers. . . . Now he would have read it. . . . Now he would be walking to the station. . . .

Perhaps Roddy had written her a letter just before he had gone away; and if so it might have come by the evening post. She left the river and went to seek it.

Who could it be coming towards her down the little pathway which led from the station to the bottom of the garden and then on to the blue gate in the wall of the garden next door? She stood still under the overhanging lilacs and may-trees, her heart pounding, her limbs melting. It was Roddy, in a white shirt and white flannels, – coming from the station. He caught sight of her, seemed to hesitate, came on till he was close to her; and she had the strangest feeling that he intended to pass right by her as if he did not see her. . . . What was the word for his face? Smooth: yes, smooth as a stone. She had never before noticed what a smooth face he had; but she could not see him clearly because of the beating of her pulses.

'Roddy!'

He lifted his eyebrows.

'Oh, hullo, Judith.'

'I thought you'd gone away.'

'I'm going to-morrow. A girl I know rang up this morning to

suggest coming down for the day, so I waited. I've just seen her off.'

A girl he knew. . . . Roddy had always had this curious facility in the dealing of verbal wounds.

'I see . . . How nice.'

A face smooth and cold as a stone. Not the faintest expression in it. Had he bidden the girl he knew good-bye with a face like this? No, it had certainly been twinkling and teasing then.

'Well I must get on.' He looked up the path as if meditating immediate escape; then said, without looking at her, and in a frozen voice: 'I got a letter from you this morning.'

'Oh you did get it?'

There could never have been a more foolish-sounding bleat. In the ensuing silence she added feebly: 'Shall you – answer it – some time?'

'I thought the best thing I could do was to leave it unanswered.'

'Oh . . .'

Because of course it had been so improper, so altogether monstrous to write like that. . . .

'Well', she said. 'I thought . . . I'm sorry.'

She ought to apologise to him, because he had meant to go away without saying anything, and she had come on him unawares and spoilt his escape.

'I was very much surprised at the way you wrote', he said.

'How do you mean, surprised, Roddy?' she said timidly.

She had known all along in the deepest layer of her consciousness that something like this would happen. Permanent happiness had never been for her.

It was not much of a shock. In a moment that night was a far, unreal memory.

'Well' – he hesitated. 'If a man wants to ask a girl to – marry him he generally asks her himself – do you see?'

'You mean – it was outrageous of me not to wait – to write like that?'

'I thought it a little odd.'

[15]

'Oh, but Roddy, surely – surely that's one of those worn-out conventions. ... Surely a woman has a perfect right to say she – loves a man – if she wants to – it's simply a question of having the courage. ... I can't see why not. ... I've always believed one should. ...'

It was no good trying to expostulate, to bluff like that, with his dead face confronting her. He would not be taken in by any such lying gallantries. How did one combat people whose features never gave way by so much as a quiver? She leaned against the wooden fence and tried to fix her eyes upon the may-tree opposite. Very far, but clear, she heard her mother at the other end of the garden, calling her name: but that was another Judith.

'I'm afraid you've misunderstood me', he said.

MARIE BASHKIRTSEFF to GUY DE MAUPASSANT

[1884]

Monsieur:

I read your works, I might almost say, with delight. In truth to nature, which you copy with religious fidelity, you find an inspiration that is truly sublime, while you move your readers by touches of feeling so profoundly human, that we fancy we see ourselves depicted in your pages, and love you with an egotistical love. Is this an unmeaning compliment? Be indulgent, it is sincere in the main.

You will understand that I should like to say many fine and striking things to you, but it is rather difficult, all at once, in this way. I regret this all the more as you are sufficiently great to inspire one with romantic dreams of becoming the confidant of your beautiful soul, always supposing your soul to be beautiful.

If your soul is not beautiful, and if 'those things are not in your line,' I shall regret it for your sake, in the first place; and in the next I shall set you down in my mind as a maker of literature, and dismiss the matter from my thoughts.

For a year past I have had the wish to write to you and was many times on the point of doing so, but – sometimes I thought I exaggerated your merits and that it was not worth while. Two days ago, however, I saw suddenly, in the *Gaulois*, that some one had honoured you with a flattering epistle and that you had inquired the address of this amiable person in order to answer him. I at once became jealous, your literary merits dazzled me anew and – here is my letter.

And now let me say that I shall always preserve my incognito for you. I do not even desire to see you from a distance – your countenance might not please me – who can tell? All I know of you now is that you are young and that you are not married, two essential points, even for a distant adoration.

But I must tell you that I am charming; this sweet reflection will stimulate you to answer my letter. It seems to me that if I were a man I should wish to hold no communication, not even an epistolary one, with an old fright of an Englishwoman, whatever might be thought by

Miss Hastings,
P.O. Station of the Madeleine

May I venture to ask you which are your favorite musicians and painters?

And how if I were a man?

KING HENRY VIII to ANNE BOLEYN

[c. 1528]

In debating with myself the contents of your letters I have been put to a great agony; not knowing how to understand them, whether to my disadvantage as shown in some places, or to my advantage as in others. I beseech you now with all my heart definitely to let me know your whole mind as to the love between us; for necessity compels me to plague you for a reply, having been for more than a year now struck by the dart of love, and being uncertain either of failure or of finding a place in your heart and affection, which point has certainly kept me for some time from naming you my mistress, since if you only love me with an ordinary love the name is not appropriate to you, seeing that it stands for an uncommon position very remote from the ordinary; but if it pleases you to do the duty of a true, loyal mistress and friend, and to give yourself body and heart to me, who have been, and will be, your very loyal servant (if your rigour does not forbid me), I promise you that not only the name will be due to you, but also to take you as my sole mistress, casting off all others than yourself out of mind and affection, and to serve you only; begging you to make me a complete reply to this my rude letter as to how far and in what I can trust; and if it does not please you to reply in writing, to let me know of some place where I can have it by word of mouth, the which place I will seek out with all my heart. No more for fear of wearying you. Written by the hand of him who would willingly remain your

HR

PLEAS

JANE WELSH CARLYLE to THOMAS CARLYLE

St. Leonards-on-Sea.
25 April, 1864

Oh my Husband! I am suffering torments! each day I suffer more horribly.

Oh, I would like you beside me! – I am terribly *alone* – But I don't want to interrupt your work. I will wait till we are in our own hired house and then if I am no better you must come for a day

Your own wretched JWC

JAMES JOYCE to NORA BARNACLE

60 Shelbourne Road
15 August 1904

My dear Nora,

It has just struck me. I came in at half past eleven. Since then I have been sitting in an easy chair like a fool. I could do nothing. I hear nothing but your voice. I am like a fool hearing you call me 'Dear.' I offended two men today by leaving them coolly. I wanted to hear your voice, not theirs.

When I am with you I leave aside my contemptuous, suspicious nature. I wish I felt your head on my shoulder. I think I will go to bed.

I have been a half-hour writing this thing. Will you write

something to me? I hope you will. How am I to sign myself? I won't sign anything at all, because I don't know what to sign myself.

STENDHAL to MADAME CURIAL

Paris, Tuesday evening, 18 May, 1824

What a sad thing adversity is, or at least how sad it makes me! I was the happiest of men or at least my heart was beating with powerful feelings when I went to your house this morning, and these feelings were sweet indeed. I spent the evening and almost the whole day with you, but with such a show of indifference that I must make an effort to convince myself that things could be otherwise. For the first time in ten years I regret having forgotten the practices of French society.

How can I see you? When will it be convenient for me to present myself again at your house? I did not go there yesterday, because a servant had seen me the day before asking the porter if you were at home. Are you satisfied with my discretion? Did I appear sufficiently unconcerned? I am angry with myself at the thought of it. For pity's sake let me know by letter the exact moments when I shall be able to find you alone. Foregoing these moments is the furthest thing from my mind at present, and I despair of ever seeing you alone in view of the number of visits which you receive.

A small signal at the window of the boudoir where you were this morning, for example, a half-closed shutter or a half-lowered blind, would tell me that I could come up. If I do not see this sign that you are alone I shall refrain from knocking on the door and will try again a quarter of an hour later.

Must it be that you will leave without my seeing you?

Rosa Luxemburg to Leo Jogiches

[6 March 1899]

I kiss you a thousand times for your dearest letter and present, though I have not yet received it. ... You simply cannot imagine how pleased I am with your choice. Why, Rodbertus is simply my favourite economist and I can read him a hundred times for sheer intellectual pleasure. ... My dear, how you delighted me with your letter. I have read it six times from beginning to end. So, you are really pleased with me. You write that perhaps I only know inside me that somewhere there is a man who belongs to me! Don't you know that everything I do is always done with you in mind; when I write an article my first thought is – this will cause you pleasure – and when I have days when I doubt my own strength and cannot work, my only fear is what effect this will have on you, that it might disappoint you. When I have proof of success, like a letter from Kautsky, this is simply my homage to you. I give you my word, as I loved my mother, that I am personally quite indifferent to what Kautsky writes. I was only pleased with it because I wrote it with your eyes and felt how much pleasure it would give you.

... Only one thing nags at my contentment: the outward arrangements of your life and of our relationship. I feel that I will soon have such an established position (morally) that we will be able to live together quite calmly, openly, as husband and wife. I am sure you understand this yourself. I am happy that the problem of your citizenship is at last coming to an end and that you are working energetically at your doctorate. I can feel from your recent letters that you are in a very good mood to work. ...

Do you think that I do not feel your value, that whenever the call to arms is sounded you always stand by me with help and encourage me to work – forgetting all the rows and all my neglect! ... You have no idea with what joy and desire I wait for every letter from you because each one brings me so much strength and happiness and encourages me to live.

I was happiest of all with that part of your letter where you write that we are both young and can still arrange our personal life. Oh darling, how I long that you may fulfil your promise. . . . Our own little room, our own furniture, a library of our own, quiet and regular work, walks together, an opera from time to time, a small – very small – circle of intimate friends who can sometimes be asked to dinner, every year a summer departure to the country for a month but definitely free from work! . . . And perhaps even a little, a very little, baby? Will this never be permitted? Never? Darling, do you know what accosted me yesterday during a walk in the park – and without any exaggeration? A little child, three or four years old, in a beautiful dress with blond hair; it stared at me and suddenly I felt an overpowering urge to kidnap the child and dash off home with him. Oh darling, will I never have my own baby?

And at home we will never argue again, will we? It must be quiet and peaceful as it is with everyone else. Only you know what worries me, I feel already so old and am not in the least attractive. You will not have an attractive wife when you walk hand in hand with her through the park – we will keep well away from the Germans. . . . Darling, if you will first settle the question of your citizenship, secondly your doctorate and thirdly live with me openly in our own room and work together with me, then we can want for nothing more! No couple on earth has so many facilities for happiness as you and I and if there is only some goodwill on our part we will be, must be, happy.

VANESSA (ESTHER VANHOMRIGH) to
JONATHAN SWIFT

Dublin, 1714

You cannot but be sensible, at least in some degree, of the many uneasinesses I am slave to – a wretch of a brother, cunning executors and importunate creditors of my mother's – things I can no way avoid being subject to at present, and weighty enough to sink greater spirits than mine without some support. Once I had a friend that would see me sometimes, and either commend what I did or advise me what to do, which banished all my uneasiness. But now, when my misfortunes are increased by being in a disagreeable place, amongst strange, prying, deceitful people, whose company is so far from an amusement that it is a very great punishment, you fly me, and give me no reason but that we are amongst fools and must submit. I am very well satisfied that we are amongst such, but know no reason for having my happiness sacrificed to their caprice. You once had a maxim, which was to act what was right and not mind what the world said. I wish you would keep to it now. Pray what can be wrong in seeing and advising an unhappy young woman? I can't imagine. You can't but know that your frowns make my life insupportable. You have taught me to distinguish, and then you leave me miserable. Now all I beg is that you will for once counterfeit (since you can't otherwise) that indulge[nt] friend you once were till I get the better of these difficulties, for my sister's sake; for were not she involved (who I know is not so able to manage them as I am), I have a nobler soul then sit struggling with misfortunes, when at the end I can't promise myself any real happiness. Forgive me; and I beg you'd believe it is not in my power to avoid complaining as I do.

JONATHAN SWIFT to
VANESSA (ESTHER VANHOMRIGH)

[c. 1714]

I received your letter when some company was with me on Saturday night; and it put me in such confusion, that I could not tell what to do. I here send you the paper you left me. This morning a woman who does business for me told me she heard I was in – with one –, naming you, and twenty particulars, that little master and I visited you, and that the Archbishop did so;

and that you had abundance of wit, etc. I ever feared the tattle of this nasty town, and told you so; and that was the reason why I said to you long ago that I would see you seldom when you were in Ireland. And I must beg you to be easy if for some time I visit you seldomer, and not in so particular a manner. I will see you at the latter end of the week if possible. These are accidents in life that are necessary and must be submitted to; and tattle, by the help of discretion, will wear off.

Monday morning, ten a clock.

VANESSA (ESTHER VANHOMRIGH) to JONATHAN SWIFT

Dublin, 1714

Well, now I plainly see how great a regard you have for me. You bid me be easy, and you'd see me as often as you could. You had better said, as often as you could get the better of your inclinations so much, or as often as you remembered there was such a one in the world. If you continue to treat me as you do you will not be made uneasy by me long. 'Tis impossible to describe what I have suffered since I saw you last; I am sure I could have bore the rack much better than those killing, killing words of yours. Sometimes I have resolved to die without seeing you more; but those resolves, to your misfortune, did not last long. For there is something in human nature that prompts one so to find relief in this world, I must give way to it, and beg you'd see me and speak kindly to me; for I am sure you'd not condemn any one to suffer what I have done, could you but know it. The reason I write to you is because I cannot tell i[t] you, should I see you; for when I begin to complain, then you are angry, and there is something in your look so awful, that it strikes me dumb. Oh! that you may but have so much regard for me left, that this complaint may touch your soul with pity. I say as little as ever I can: did you but know

[26]

what I thought, I am sure it would move you. Forgive me, and
believe I cannot help telling you this, and live.

THEON to THEON his father

[Second century, Roman]
Theon to Theon his father, greeting. That was a fine trick, not
taking me to the city with you! If you don't take me to Alexandria
with you, I won't write to you! I won't speak to you! I won't wish
you good-morning! If you do go to Alexandria, I won't hold your
hand or have anything more to say to you. That's what will
happen if you don't take me! Mother said to Archelaus, 'Take him
out of my way, he upsets me'. That was a fine thing you did, to
send that fine present of beans! They kept me in the dark at home
on the 12th when you sailed. Please send for me. If you don't I
won't eat or drink. Goodbye.

Oxyrhynchus Papyri CXIX.

REJECTIONS

VINCENT to ANNA in *Voyage in the Dark* by Jean Rhys

My dear Anna,

This is a very difficult letter to write because I am afraid I am going to upset you and I hate upsetting people. We've been back for nearly a week but Walter hasn't been at all well and I have persuaded him to let me write to you and explain matters. I'm quite sure you are a nice girl and that you will be understanding about this. Walter is still very fond of you but he doesn't love you like that any more, and after all you must always have known that the thing could not go on for ever and you must remember too that he is nearly twenty years older than you are. I'm sure that you are a nice girl and that you will think it over calmly and see that there is nothing to be tragic or unhappy or anything like that about. You are young and youth as everybody says is the great thing, the greatest gift of all. The greatest gift, everybody says. And so it is. You've got everything in front of you, lots of happiness. Think of that. Love is not everything – especially that sort of love – and the more people, especially girls, put it right out of their heads and do without it the better. That's my opinion. Life is chock-full of other things, my dear girl, friends and just good times and being jolly together and so on and games and books. Do you remember when we talked about books? I was sorry when you told me that you never read because, believe me, a good book like that book I was talking about can make a lot of difference to your point of view. It makes you see what is real and what is just imaginary. My dear Infant, I am writing this in the country, and I can assure you that when you get into a garden and smell the flowers and all that all this rather beastly sort of love simply doesn't matter. However, you will think I'm preaching at you, so I will shut up. These muddles do happen. They have happened to me, as a matter of fact, worse luck. I can't think why. I can't think why one can't be more sensible. However, I have learnt one thing, that it never helps to let things drag on. Walter has asked me to enclose this cheque for £20 for your immediate expenses because he thinks you may be running short of cash. He will always be your friend and he wants to arrange that you should be provided for and not have to worry about money (for a time at any rate). Write and let him know that you understand. If you really care for him at all you will do this, for believe me he is unhappy about you and he has a lot of other worries as well. Or write me – that would be better still because don't you think it would be just as well for both your sakes if you don't see Walter just now? Then there's that job in the new show. I want to take you along as soon as possible to see my friend. I think I can promise you that something will come of it. I believe that if you will work hard there is no reason why you should not get on. I've always said that and I stick to it.

Yours ever,
Vincent Jeffries.

P.S. Have you kept any of the letters Walter wrote to you? If so you ought to send them back.

After a while I crossed out everything and began again, writing very quickly, like you do when you write: 'You can't possibly do this you simply don't know what you're doing if I were a dog you wouldn't do this I love you I love you I love you but you're just a goddamned rotter everybody is everybody is everybody is. My dear Walter I've read books about this and I know quite well what you're thinking but you're quite wrong because don't you remember you used to joke because every time you put your hand on my heart it used to jump well you can't pretend that can you you can pretend everything else but not that it's the only thing you can't pretend I do want to ask you one thing I'd like to see you just once more listen it needn't be for very long it need only be for

an hour well not an hour then half an hour . . .' And going on like
that, and the sheets of paper all over the bed.

(DORA) CARRINGTON to MARK GERTLER

Ibthorpe House, Hurstbourne Tarrant,
nr Andover, Hants
16 April, 1915

NEXT LETTER. WHEN YOU WRITE, WHENEVER YOU DO *DON'T*
MENTION OUR SEX TROUBLE ETC ETC ETC: *AT ALL* I AM
HEARTILY SICK OF IT — JUST WRITE AND TELL ME ABOUT
YOURSELF THE COUNTRY AS USUAL. AND IF EVER I WRITE ABOUT
IT TO YOU, *PLEASE* TAKE NO NOTICE.

OUR FRIENDSHIP IS NO WORSE OR BETTER THAN ANY OTHER
FRIENDSHIP. AT ANY RATE WE ARE INTERESTED IN EACH OTHER
— ENOUGH. WHY SHOULD WE FUSS?

I WANT *SIMPLY* YOUR *FRIENDSHIP* AND *COMPANY* MORE
THAN ANYTHING IN THE WORLD. *

You wrote these last lines only a week ago, and now you tell me
you were *'hysterical and insincere'.* When you talked [to] me about
it at Gilbert's and said you loved my friendship were you hysterical and insincere? Yes I know that your real love is 'beautiful
and not low'. Do not think I ever doubted that.

Only I *cannot* love you as you want me to. You must know one
could not do, what you ask, sexual intercourse, unless one does
love a man's body. I have never felt any desire for that in my life: I
wrote only four months ago and told you all this, you said you
never wanted me to take any notice of you when you wrote again;
if it was not that you just asked me to speak frankly and plainly I

---

* The capitalized passages in the above letter were cut out of a letter from Gertler to
Carrington and pasted on to her letter to him.

should not be writing. I do love you, but not in the way you want. Once, you made love to me in your studio, you remember, many years ago now. One thing I can never forget, it made me inside feel ashamed, unclean. Can I help it? I wish to God I could. Do not think I rejoice in being sexless, and am happy over this. It gives me pain also.

Whenever you feel you want my friendship and company, it will *always* be here. You know that. This is all I can say.

REMEMBER THAT I WOULD SACRIFICE ALL FOR YOU, MY VERY LIFE IF YOU ASKED IT OF ME.

You write this – yet you cannot sacrifice something *less than your life* for me. I do not ask it of you. But it would make me happy if you could. Do not be angry with me for having written as I have. And please do not write back. There can be nothing more to say. Unless you can make this one sacrifice for me. I will do everything I can to be worthy of it.

NINON DE LENCLOS to the MARQUIS DE SÉVIGNÉ

[*c.* 1650]

Yes, Marquis, I will keep my word with you, and upon all occasions shall speak the truth, though I sometimes tell it at my own expense. I have more firmness of mind than perhaps you may imagine, and 'tis very probable that in the course of this correspondence, you will think I push this quality too far, even to severity. But then, please to remember that I have only the outside of a woman, and that my heart and mind are wholly masculine. . . .

Shall I tell you what makes love so dangerous? 'Tis the too high idea we are apt to form of it. But to speak the truth, love, considered as a passion, is merely a blind instinct, that we should rate accordingly. It is an appetite, which inclines us to one object, rather than another, without our being able to account for our taste. Considered as a bond of friendship, where reason presides, it is no longer a passion and loses the very name of love. It becomes esteem: which is indeed a very pleasing appetite, but too tranquil; and therefore incapable of rousing you from your present supineness.

If you madly trace the footsteps of our ancient heroes of romance, adopting their extravagant sentiments, you will soon experience, that such false chivalry metamorphoses this charming passion into a melancholy folly; nay, often a tragical one: a perfect frenzy! but divest it of all the borrowed pomp of opinion, and you will then perceive how much it will contribute both to your happiness and pleasure. Be assured that if either reason or knight-errantry should be permitted to form the union of our hearts, love would become a state of apathy and madness.

The only way to avoid these extremes, is to pursue the course I pointed out to you. At present you have no occasion for any thing more than mere amusement, and believe me, you will not meet it except among women of the character I speak of. Your heart wants occupation; and they are framed to supply the void. At least, give my prescription a fair trial, and I will be answerable for the success.

I promised to reason with you, and I think I have kept my word. Farewell. . . .

To-morrow the Abbé Chateauneuf, and perhaps Molière are to be with me. We are to read over the *Tartuffe* together, in order to make some necessary alterations. Depend upon it, Marquis, that whoever denies the maxims I have here laid down, partakes a little of that character in his play.

[Chavaniac, 27 March 1783]

You are too cruel, my dear Aglaé. You realize my heart's torments. You know that it is torn between love and duty, and you insist that it pronounce a decision upon that miserable resolution. You have seen me make so many that I did not have the strength to keep. A hundred times I considered the last word said, the final promise made; a hundred times I have put myself under obligation in regard to you, and a hundred times the instant I saw you and touched you proved too well how weak I am. I did not see your mother. I looked for her, however, but without being sorry not to find her. Her arguments are so good, and they are so contrary to my heart's desire. When I came back from America, my lovable dear, was it you, or was it I who did the preaching on the way we had of being together? Do you remember my insistence, your refusals, our quarrels. I accused you of repugnance, you accused me of lacking delicacy. Our quarrels ended like all lovers' quarrels, but although carried away by my passion, I would recall both the reproaches of your relatives and the efforts that I was making to win you. Every day renewed resistance, and in consequence new regrets. I was happy, however, it must be admitted, but you were not, and it is you who risk everything while I get nearly all the pleasure. You consented hardly a single time without resistance, and the last decisions which you have made are a constant reproach to my lack of delicacy. At every moment you ruin your life for me, and to make me appreciate it the more, you refuse to share what I feel. And you still demand that I decide? Ah, you know only too well my passion, my transport, my entire abandon. You have too often beheld my struggles and my weakness. You have known me; you have loved me in every respect; but you have never known me to be generous except in contemplation, and whatever it may cost me, I want if I can to be so once in reality.

It is over a year that you have endeavored to break this sort of tie. Every day has seen your efforts redouble. Every day you have had to stand for either a display of temperament or of violence. Now you are taking a final course; it is the cruelest for me, but it is the only one that might succeed, and the only question is to find out whether I am a decent man. You put in my hands your peace of mind, your safety, and much more, as you know. I do not mention your family, since I would not give up so much happiness for anyone else in the world. You understand the extent of my sacrifice. You have often seen me grow pale merely at the idea of that reconciliation. But after all, for a year, I have seen that there was something more at stake than my happiness. I will silence my heart, and as you have wisely predicted, I am more master of myself in a letter than in a conversation. It would have been kinder not to have given me the pain of deciding, but since you have wished it so, rest assured, my dear, that my heart is delicate though passionate. So be it.

I laid my pen aside for a long time before writing those words. But after all, it is your wish, and that of your family. Your whole existence depends on it. What need did you have of my opinion? Can a decent man advise you to ruin your life? No, my dear, and whatever it may cost me, I advise what reason tells you, and decency imposes upon me.

In coming to this conclusion, my dear, I fully realize how repugnant it all is. I well appreciate that only my opinion is needed and that you keenly wish for this decision. For if there were not so acute a danger, you would not place upon me the horror of a decision. Such vile coquetry is so far from the nobility of your sentiments. May you find peace, since we are not to be happy. There you are then at the point where, for a year, you have wanted to be.

As to the nonsense people tell you, I do not care to take those feeble weapons away from your family. You know yourself, and some day you will know better yet what these weapons are. But at least my heart is my own, dear Aglaé. All that you are, all that I owe to you, justifies my love, and nothing, not even you, would keep me from adoring you.

[37]

JEAN JACQUES ROUSSEAU to COUNTESS SOPHIE D'HOUDETOT

Eremitage, June 1757

Come, Sophie, that I may torture your unjust heart in order that I, on my side, may be merciless towards you. Why should I spare you, whilst you rob me of reason, of honour, and life? Why should I allow your days to pass in peace, you, who make mine unbearable! – Ah, much less cruel would you have been, if you had driven a dagger into my heart, instead of the fateful weapon, which kills me! Look what I was and what I am now; look to what a degree you have abased me. When you deigned to be mine, I was more than a man; since you have driven me from you, I am the least of mortals. I have lost all reason, all understanding, and all courage; in a word, you have taken everything from me! How could you determine to destroy your own handiwork? How can you dare to consider him as unworthy of esteem, whom you honoured once with your graciousness? Ah, Sophie, I beseech you, do not be ashamed of a friend, whom you once favoured. For your own honour I demand you to render me an account of myself. Am I not your property? Have you not taken possession of me? That you cannot deny, and as I belong to you in spite of myself and of yourself, so let me at least deserve to be yours. Think of those times of happiness, which, to my torture, I shall never forget. That invisible flame from which I received a second, more precious life, rendered to my soul and my senses the whole force of youth. The glow of my feelings raised me to you. How often was not your heart, filled with love for another, touched by the passion of mine. How often did you not say to me in the grove by the waterfall, 'You are the most tender lover, that I can imagine; no, never did a man love like you!' What a triumph for me, such a confession from your lips! Yes, it was real! it was worthy of the passion from which I demanded so ardently, that it should make you receptive, and with which I wished to awake in you a compassion that you now regret so bitterly. . . .

O Sophie! after all the sweet moments the thought of an eternal renunciation is terrible for him, whom it saddens deeply that he cannot identify himself with you. What! your touching eyes will never droop again before my glances with that sweet shame, which so intoxicated me with sensuous desire? I am never more to feel that heavenly shudder, that maddening, devouring fire, which quicker than lightning ... oh, inexpressible moment! What heart, what god could have experienced you and resisted?

ROBERT DE MONTESQUIOU to JEAN COUCHAUD
from *Prince of Aesthetes: Count Robert de Montesquiou*
by Philippe Jullian

[1914]
'. . . You have come out of the mystery that shrouded you and have put me in the presence of a correct, reserved, circumspect and cold young man, whose harsh voice surprised me on the telephone and whom I was subsequently disconcerted to meet in a spiritless reality. That visit, which you offered to pay me when I did not know you, you no longer offered me when it seemed to be indicated, and thus the misunderstandings of proud souls have begun to weave their invisible but not unfeeling web.' After that the correspondence dragged, the misapprehensions multiplied, and the last letter, written four months before the death of the poet, as his final bouquet offered up to Beauty, has the bitter odour of the dust: 'From the time that I loved you without knowing you, I would have been moved to wander over places:
Honoured by the steps and lit by the eyes
Of the charming young shepherd.
Today I only see the graceless vista of a place both unattractive and dry.'

Letter of the FAIR MAID OF ASTOLAT
in *Le Morte d'Arthur* by Sir Thomas Malory

... And then she called her father, Sir Bernard, and her brother, Sir Tirre, and heartily she prayed her father that her brother might write a letter like as she did indite it: and so her father granted her. And when the letter was written word by word like as she devised then she prayed her father that she might be watched until she were dead. And while my body is hot let this letter be put in my right hand, and my hand bound fast with the letter until that I be cold; and let me be put in a fair bed with all the richest clothes that I have about me, and so let my bed and all my richest clothes be laid with me in a chariot unto the next place where Thames is; and there let me be put within a barget, and but one man with me, such as ye trust to steer me thither, and that my barget be covered with black samite over and over: thus father I beseech you let it be done ...

So by fortune King Arthur and Queen Guenever were speaking together at a window, and so as they looked into Thames they espied this black barget, and had marvel what it meant ...

Then the king made the barget to be holden fast, and then the king and queen entered with certain knights with them; and there he saw the fairest woman lie in a rich bed, covered unto her middle with many rich clothes, and all was of cloth of gold, and she lay as though she had smiled. Then the queen espied a letter in her right hand, and told it to the king. Then the king took it and said: Now am I sure this letter will tell what she was, and why she is come hither. So then the king and queen went out of the barget, and so commanded a certain man to wait upon the barget. And so when the king was come within his chamber, he called many knights about him, and said that he would wit openly what was written within that letter. Then the king brake it, and made a clerk to read it, and this was the intent of the letter.

Most noble knight, Sir Launcelot, now hath death made us two at debate for your love. I was your lover, that men called the fair maiden of Astolat; therefore unto all ladies I make my moan, yet pray for my soul and bury me at least, and offer ye my mass-penny: this is my last request. And a clene maiden I died, I take God to witness: pray for my soul, Sir Launcelot, as thou art peerless. This is all the substance of the letter. And when it was read, the king, the queen, and all the knights wept for pity of the doleful complaints.

FEARS AND
WORRIES

JAMES JOYCE to NORA BARNACLE

60 Shelbourne Road

29 August 1904

My dear Nora

I have just finished my midnight dinner for which I had no appetite. When I was half way through it I discovered I was eating it out of my fingers. I felt sick just as I did last night. I am much distressed. Excuse this dreadful pen and this awful paper.

I may have pained you tonight by what I said but surely it is well that you should know my mind on most things? My mind rejects the whole present social order and Christianity – home, the recognised virtues, classes of life, and religious doctrines. How could I like the idea of home? My home was simply a middle-class affair ruined by spendthrift habits, which I have inherited. My mother was slowly killed, I think, by my father's ill-treatment, by years of trouble, and by my cynical frankness of conduct. When I looked on her face as she lay in her coffin – a face grey and wasted with cancer – I understood that I was looking on the face of a victim and I cursed the system which had made her a victim. We were seventeen in family. My brothers and sisters are nothing to me. One brother alone is capable of understanding me.

Six years ago I left the Catholic Church, hating it most fervently. I found it impossible for me to remain in it on account of the impulses of my nature. I made secret war upon it when I was a student and declined to accept the positions it offered me. By doing this I made myself a beggar but I retained my pride. Now I make open war upon it by what I write and say and do. I cannot enter the social order except as a vagabond. I started to study

[45]

medicine three times, law once, music once. A week ago I was arranging to get away as a travelling actor. I could put no energy into the plan because you kept pulling me by the elbow. The actual difficulties of my life are incredible but I despise them.

When you went in tonight I wandered along towards Grafton St where I stood for a long time leaning against a lamp-post, smoking. The street was full of a life which I have poured a stream of my youth upon. While I stood there I thought of a few sentences I wrote some years ago when I lived in Paris – these sentences which follow – 'They pass in twos and threes, amid the life of the boulevard, walking like people who have leisure in a place lit up for them. They are in the pastry cook's, chattering, crushing little fabrics of pastry, or seated silently at tables by the café door, or descending from carriages with a busy stir of garments soft as the voice of the adulterer. They pass in air of perfumes. Under the perfumes their bodies have a warm humid smell' –.

While I was repeating this to myself I knew that that life was still waiting for me if I chose to enter it. It could not give me perhaps the intoxication it had once given but it was still there and now that I am wiser but more controllable it was safe. It would ask no questions, expect nothing from me but a few moments of my life, leaving the rest free, and would promise me pleasure in return. I thought of all this and without regret I rejected it. It was useless for me; it would not give me what I wanted.

You have misunderstood, I think, some passages in a letter I wrote you and I have noticed a certain shyness in your manner as if the recollection of that night [June 16] troubled you. I however consider it a kind of sacrament and the recollection of it fills me with amazed joy. You will perhaps not understand at once why it is that I honour you so much on account of it as you do not know much of my mind. But at the same time it was a sacrament which left in me a final sense of sorrow and degradation – sorrow because I saw in you an extraordinary, melancholy tenderness which had chosen that sacrament as a compromise, and

[46]

degradation because I understood that in your eyes I was inferior to a convention of our present society.

I spoke to you satirically tonight but I was speaking of the world not of you. I am an enemy of the ignobleness and slavishness of people but not of you. Can you not see the simplicity which is at the back of all my disguises? We all wear masks. Certain people who know that we are much together often insult me about you. I listen to them calmly, disdaining to answer them but their least word tumbles my heart about like a bird in a storm.

It is not pleasant to me that I have to go to bed now, remembering the last look of your eyes – a look of tired indifference – remembering the torture of your voice the other night. No human being has ever stood so close to my soul as you stand, it seems, and yet you can treat my words with painful rudeness ('I know what is talking now' you said). When I was younger I had a friend [Byrne] to whom I gave myself freely – in a way more than I give to you and in a way less. He was Irish, that is to say, he was false to me.

I have not said a quarter of what I want to say but it is great labour writing with this cursed pen. I don't know what you will think of this letter. Please write to me, won't you? Believe me, my dear Nora, I honour you very much but I want more than your caresses. You have left me again in an anguish of doubt.

JAJ

Count Gabriel Honoré de Mirabeau to Sophie de Monnier

[c. 1780]

To be with the people one loves, says La Bruyère, is enough – to dream you are speaking to them, not speaking to them, thinking of them, thinking of the most indifferent things, but by their side, nothing else matters. O mon amie, how true that is! and it is also true that when one acquires such a habit, it becomes a necessary part of one's existence. Alas! I well know, I should know too well, since the three months that I sigh, far away from thee, that I possess thee no more, that my happiness has departed. However, when every morning I wake up, I look for you, it seems to me that half of myself is missing, and that is too true. Twenty times during the day, I ask myself where you are; judge how strong the illusion is, and how cruel it is to see it vanish. When I go to bed, I do not fail to make room for you; I push myself quite close to the wall and leave a great empty space in my small bed. This movement is mechanical, these thoughts are involuntary. Ah! how one accustoms oneself to happiness. Alas! one only knows it well when one has lost it, and I am sure we have only learnt to appreciate how necessary we are to each other, since the thunderbolt has parted us. The source of our tears has not dried up, dear Sophie; we cannot become healed; we have enough in our hearts to love always, and, because of that, enough to weep always. Let those prate who affirm that they have shaken off a great affliction by virtue or by strength of mind; they only became consoled because they are weak and on the surface. There are losses one must never be reconciled to; and when one can no longer bring happiness to what one loves, then one must bring misfortune. Let us speak the Truth itself, it must be; and this delicate sentiment, whatever one may say, is in the nature of a tender love. Would Sophie not be in despair, if she knew her Gabriel consoled?

ZELDA FITZGERALD to F. SCOTT FITZGERALD

[Spring 1919]

Sweetheart,

   Please, please don't be so depressed – We'll be married soon, and then these lonesome nights will be over forever – and until we are, I am loving, loving every tiny minute of the day and night – Maybe you won't understand this, but sometimes when I miss you most, it's hardest to write – and you always know when I make myself – Just the ache of it all – and I *can't* tell you. If we were together, you'd feel how strong it is – you're so sweet when you're melancholy. I love your sad tenderness – when I've hurt you – That's one of the reasons I could never be sorry for our quarrels – and they bothered you so – Those dear, dear little fusses, when I always tried so hard to make you kiss and forget –

Scott – there's nothing in all the world I want but you – and your precious love – All the material things are nothing. I'd just hate to live a sordid, colorless existence – because you'd soon love me less – and less – and I'd do anything – anything – to keep your heart for my own – I don't want to live – I want to love first, and live incidentally – Why don't you feel that I'm waiting – I'll come to you, Lover, when you're ready – Don't – don't ever think of the things you can't give me – You've trusted me with the dearest heart of all – and it's so damn much more than anybody else in all the world has ever had –

How can you think deliberately of life without me – If you should die – O Darling – darling [Scott] – It'd be like going blind. I know I would, too, – I'd have no purpose in life – just a pretty – decoration. Don't you think I was made for you? I feel like you had me ordered – and I was delivered to you – to be worn – I want you to wear me, like a watch – charm or a button hole [bouquet] – to the world. And then, when we're alone, I want to help – to know that you can't do *anything* without me.

I'm glad you wrote Mamma. It was such a nice sincere letter – and mine to St Paul was very evasive and rambling. I've never, in all my life, been able to say anything to people older than me – Somehow I just instinctively avoid personal things with them – even my family. Kids are so much nicer.

MICHAEL FARADAY to SARAH BARNARD

[December 1820]
Royal Institution. Thursday evening.
My Dear Sarah – It is astonishing how much the state of the body influences the powers of the mind. I have been thinking all the morning of the very delightful and interesting letter I would send you this evening, and now I am so tired, and yet have so much to do, that my thoughts are quite giddy, and run round your image without any power of themselves to stop and admire it. I want to say a thousand kind and, believe me, heartfelt things to you, but am not master of words fit for the purpose; and still, as I ponder and think on you, chlorides, trials, oil, Davy, steel, miscellanea, mercury, and fifty other professional fancies swim before and drive me further and further into the quandary of stupidness.

From your affectionate
Michael

MARGERY BREWS to SIR JOHN PASTON

[February 1477]
Unto my right well-beloved Valentine, John Paston,
Esquire, be this bill delivered, etc.

Right reverend and worshipful, and my right well-beloved Valentine, I recommend me unto you, full heartily desiring to hear of your welfare, which I beseech Almighty God long for to preserve unto His pleasure and your heart's desire.

And if it please you to hear of my welfare, I am not in good health of body nor of heart, nor shall be till I hear from you;

For there wots no creature what pain that I endure,
And for to be dead, I dare it not discur.

And my lady my mother hath laboured the matter to my father

full diligently; but she can no more get than ye know of, for the which God knoweth I am full sorry. But if that ye love me, as I trust verily that ye do, ye will not leave me therefore; for if that ye had not half the livelode that ye have, for to do the greatest labour that any woman alive might, I would not forsake you.

And if ye command me to keep me true wherever I go,
I wis I will do all my might you to love, and never no mo.
And if my friends say that I do amiss,
They shall not me let so for to do,
Mine heart me bids evermore to love you
Truly over all earthly thing,
And if they be never so wrath,
I trust it shall be better in time coming.

No more to you at this time, but the Holy Trinity have you in keeping. And I beseech you that this bill be not seen of none earthly creature save only yourself, etc.

And this letter was endited at Topcroft, with full heavy heart, etc.

By your own
Margery Brews.

QUEEN MARY II to KING WILLIAM III

[1690]
Whitehall, September.

... I never do anything now without thinking, it may be, you are in the greatest dangers, and yet I must see company upon my set days. I must play twice a-week – nay, I must laugh and talk, though never so much against my will. I believe I dissemble very ill to those who know me, – at least, 'tis a good constraint to myself, yet I must endure it. All my motions are so watched, and all I do so observed, that if I eat less, or speak less, or look more grave, all is lost in the opinion of the world. So that I have this misery added to that of your absence and my fears for your dear person, that I must grin when my heart is ready to break, and talk when it is so oppressed I can scarce breathe.

I don't know what I should do, were it not for the Grace of God, which supports me. I am sure I have great reason to praise the Lord while I live, for His great mercy that I don't sink under this affliction, nay, that I keep my health, for I can neither sleep nor eat. I go to Kensington as often as I can for air, but then I can never be quite alone; neither can I complain, – that would be some ease; but I have nobody whose humour and circumstances agree with mine enough to speak my mind freely. Besides, I must hear of business, which, being a thing I am so new in, and so unfit for, does but break my brains the more, and not ease my heart. I see I have insensibly made my letter too long upon my own self, but I am confident you love enough to bear it for once. I don't remember I have been guilty of the like fault before, since you went, and that is now three months; for which time of almost perpetual fear and trouble this is but a short account, and so I hope may pass.

'T is some ease to me to write my pain, and 't is some satisfaction to believe you will pity me. It will be yet more when I hear it from yourself in a letter, as I am sure you must, if it be but out of common good-nature; how much more, then, out of kindness, if you love me as well as you make me believe, and as I endeavour to deserve a little by that sincere and lasting kindness I have for you. But, by making excuses, I do but take up more of your time, and therefore I must tell you that this morning Lord Marlborough went away. As little reason as I have to care for his wife, yet I must pity her condition, having lain-in but eight days; and I have great compassion for wives, when their husbands go to fight.

I have almost forgot to tell you, that in the *Utrecht Courant* they have printed a letter of yours to the States of Holland, in which you promise to be soon with them. I can't tell you how many ill hours I have had about that, in the midst of my joy when I thought you were coming home, for it troubled me to think you would go over and fight again there.

Henrik Ibsen to Emilie Bardach

[6 February 1890]

Long, very long, have I left your last, dear letter – read and read again – without an answer. Take today my heartfelt thanks for it, though given in very few words. Henceforth, till we see each other face to face, you will hear little from me, and very seldom. Believe me, it is better so. It is the only right thing. It is a matter of conscience with me to end our correspondence, or at least to limit it. You yourself should have as little to do with me as possible. With your young life you have other aims to follow, other tasks to fulfil. And I – I have told you so already – can never be content with a mere exchange of letters. For me it is only half the thing; it is a false situation. Not to give myself wholly and unreservedly makes me unhappy. It is my nature. I cannot change it. You are so delicately subtle, so instinctively penetrating, that you will easily see what I mean. When we are together again, I shall be able to explain it more fully. Till then, and always, you will be in my thoughts. You will be so even more when we no longer have to stop at this wearisome halfway house of correspondence. A thousand greetings.

Your

H.I.

Emilie Bardach to Henrik Ibsen

[7 February 1890]

Please forgive me for writing again so soon. All these days I have been intending to write to you, for it is part of my nature to feel anxious about persons to whom I am deeply attached if I do not hear from them for a longish while. Possibly this is a petty characteristic, but it is impossible to control one's feelings. Nevertheless, I mean to control mine, and since I know how

[53]

sensitive you are in this respect I came halfway to meet you. Yes, I knew very well that you are an unwilling letter-writer, and from time to time I even felt that you might find my letters a nuisance. All the same, your last letter has shaken me badly, and I have needed all my self-control to conceal my feelings. But I don't want this to prevent you from carrying out your intentions. I certainly do not wish you to write to me frequently, and since you wish it I shall also refrain. However, I cannot allow myself to prescribe the problems and the moods to which, as you say, I should surrender myself in my young life. What I have so often told you remains unaltered and I can never forget it. Unfortunately the fact remains that I cannot surrender myself completely, nor taste unalloyed enjoyment. Forgive me for drawing you into a conflict with fate. That is ungrateful of me, seeing that you have so often said to me that whatever happens we shall remain good friends, and that I must hold fast to that. And is it friendship not to know if the other is ill or well, happy or wretched? And then can I prevent the thought coming to me that *you* want to avoid seeing me again, and anyhow, if you do not write, how am I to know where we can find each other again? Well, I'll be very, very patient; I can wait, but I shall suffer very much if I don't get a line or a book from you from time to time, or some other proof that you think of me. I am not noble enough to dispense with such little proofs of your interest.

Ought I to be ashamed of my frankness? Will you think less of me for not wishing to give up what has made me so happy and more contented through all these months? I know you a little and that is why I understand so much that is in you, but I am sure that *your conscience* should never hinder you from continuing to write to me. By so doing you only show your kindness. I will try to understand all other reasons that may prevent you from writing and certainly I don't want you to act against your feelings. What a multitude of things there are to write about, but you do not wish me to write, even though I should not expect an answer.

Tonight I have an invitation to a ball – with friends; I never go out in public. When I am there I shall allow myself to think a little about you because I often find parties like these extremely uninspiring, unless I have something of my own to fall back on. Anyhow, I mean to go, if I can.

With love

Emilie.

DOROTHY OSBORNE to WILLIAM TEMPLE

[c. 1652–4]

Sir,

Having tired myself with thinking, I mean to weary you with reading, and revenge myself that way for all the unquiet thoughts you have given me. But I intended this a sober letter, and therefore, *sans raillerie*, let me tell you, I have seriously considered all our misfortunes, and can see no end of them but by submitting to that which we cannot avoid, and by yielding to it break the force of a blow which if resisted brings a certain ruin. I think I need not tell you how dear you have been to me, nor that in your kindness I placed all the satisfaction of my life; 'twas the only happiness I proposed to myself, and had set my heart so much upon it that it was therefore made my punishment, to let me see that, how innocent soever I thought my affection, it was guilty in being greater than is allowable for things of this world. 'Tis not a melancholy humour gives me these apprehensions and inclinations, nor the persuasions of others; 'tis the result of a long strife with myself, before my reason could overcome my passion, or bring me to a perfect resignation to whatsoever is allotted for me. 'Tis now done, I hope, and I have nothing left but to persuade you to that, which I assure myself your own judgment will approve in the end, and your reason has often prevailed with you to offer; that which you would have done then out of kindness to me and point of honour, I would have you do now out of wisdom and kindness to yourself. Not that I would disclaim my part in it or lessen my obligation to you, no, I am your friend as much as ever I was in my life, I think more, and am sure I shall never be less. I have known you long enough to discern that you have all the qualities that make an excellent friend, and I shall endeavour to deserve that you may be so to me; but I would have you do this upon the justest grounds, and such as may conduce most to your quiet and future satisfaction. When we have tried all ways to happiness, there is no such thing to be found but in a mind conformed to one's condition, whatsoever it be, and in not aiming at anything that is either impossible or improbable; all the rest is but vanity and vexation of spirit, and I durst pronounce it so from that little knowledge I have had of the world, though I had not Scripture for my warrant. The shepherd that bragged to the traveller, who asked him. 'What weather it was like to be?' that it should be what weather pleased him, and made it good by saying it should be what weather pleased God, and what pleased God should please him, said an excellent thing in rude language, and knew enough to make him the happiest person in the world if he made a right use on't. There can be no pleasure in a struggling life, and that folly which we condemn in an ambitious man, that's ever labouring for that which is hardly got and more uncertainly kept, is seen in all according to their several humours; in some 'tis covetousness, in others pride, in some a stubbornness of nature that chooses to go always against the tide, and in others an unfortunate fancy to things that are in themselves innocent till we make them otherwise by desiring them too much. Of this sort I think you, and I, are; we have lived hitherto upon hopes so airy that I have often wondered how they could support the weight of our misfortunes; but passion gives a strength above nature, we see it in mad people; and, not to flatter ourselves, ours is but a refined degree of madness. What can it be else to be lost to all things in the world but that single object that takes up one's fancy, to lose all the quiet and repose of one's life in hunting after it, when there is so little likelihood of ever gaining it, and so many more probable accidents that will infallibly make us miss of it? And, which is more than all, 'tis being mastered by that which reason and religion teaches us to govern, and in that only gives us a preeminence above beasts. This, soberly consider'd, is enough to let us see our error, and consequently to persuade us to redeem it. To another person, I should justify myself that 'tis not a lightness in my nature, nor any interest that is not common to us both, that has wrought this change in me. To you that know my heart, and from whom I shall never hide it, to whom a thousand testimonies of my kindness can witness the reality of it, and whose friendship is not built upon common grounds, I have no more to say but that I impose not my opinions upon you, and that I had rather you took them up as your own choice than upon my entreaty. But if, as we have not differed in anything else, we could agree in this too, and resolve upon a friendship that will be much the perfecter for having nothing of passion in it, how happy might we be without so much as a fear of the change that any accident could bring. We might defy all that fortune could do, and putting off all disguise and constraint, with that which only made it necessary, make our lives as easy to us as the condition of this world will permit. I may own you as a person that I extremely value and esteem, and for whom I have a particular friendship, and you may consider me as one that will always be

Your faithful.

ECSTASIES

VICTOR HUGO to ADÈLE FOUCHER

Friday evening, March 15th, 1822

After the two delightful evenings spent yesterday and the day before, I shall certainly not go out to-night, but will sit here at home and write to you. Besides, my Adèle, my adorable and adored Adèle, what have I not to tell you? O, God! for two days, I have been asking myself every moment if such happiness is not a dream. It seems to me that what I feel is not of earth. I cannot yet comprehend this cloudless heaven.

You do not yet know, Adèle, to what I had resigned myself. Alas! do I know it myself? Because I was weak, I fancied I was calm; because I was preparing myself for all the mad follies of despair, I thought I was courageous and resigned. Ah! let me cast myself humbly at your feet, you who are so grand, so tender and so strong! I had been thinking that the utmost limit of my devotion could only be the sacrifice of my life; but *you*, my generous love, were ready to sacrifice for me the repose of yours.

Adèle, to what follies, what delirium, did not your Victor give way during these everlasting eight days! Sometimes I was ready to accept the offer of your admirable love; I thought that if pushed to the last extremity by the letter from my father, I might realize a little money, and then carry you away – *you*, my betrothed, my companion, my wife – away from all those who might want to disunite us; I thought we could cross France, I being nominally your husband, and go into some other country which would give us our rights. By day we would travel in the same carriage, by night sleep under the same roof.

But do not think, my noble Adèle, that I would have taken

advantage of so much happiness. Is it not true that you would never have done me the dishonour of thinking so? You would have been the object most worthy of respect, the being most respected, by your Victor; you might on the journey have even slept in the same chamber without fearing that he would have alarmed you by a touch, or even have looked at you. Only I should have slept, or watched wakefully in a chair, or lying on the floor beside your bed, the guardian of your repose, the protector of your slumbers. The right to defend and to watch over you would have been the only one of a husband's rights that your slave would have aspired to, until a priest had given him all the others. . . .

Adèle, oh! do not hate me, do not despise me for having been so weak and abject when you were so strong and so sublime. Think of my bereavement, of my loneliness, of what I expected from my father; think that for a week I had looked forward to losing you, and do not be astonished at the extravagance of my despair. You – a young girl – were admirable. And indeed, I feel as if it would be flattering an angel to compare such a being to you. You have been privileged to receive every gift from nature, you have both fortitude and tears. Oh, Adèle, do not mistake these words for blind enthusiasm – enthusiasm for you has lasted all my life, and increases day by day. My whole soul is yours. If my entire existence had not been yours, the harmony of my being would have been lost, and I must have died – died inevitably.

These were my meditations, Adèle, when the letter that was to bring me hope or else despair arrived. If you love me, you know what must have been my joy. What I know you may have felt, I will not describe.

My Adèle, why is there no word for this but joy? Is it because there is no power in human speech to express such happiness?

The sudden bound from mournful resignation to infinite felicity seemed to upset me. Even now I am still beside myself and sometimes I tremble lest I should suddenly awaken from this dream divine.

Oh, now you are mine! At last you are mine! Soon – in a few

months, perhaps, my angel will sleep in my arms, will awaken in my arms, will live there. All your thoughts at all moments, all your looks will be for me; all my thoughts, all my moments, all my looks, will be for you! My Adèle! . . .

And now you will belong to me! Now I am called on earth to enjoy celestial felicity. I see you as my young wife, then a young mother, but always the same, always my Adèle, as tender, as adored in the chastity of married life as in the virgin days of your first love – Dear love, answer me – tell me if you can conceive the happiness of love immortal in an eternal union! And that will be ours some day. . . .

My Adèle, no obstacle will now discourage me, either in my writing or in my attempt to gain a pension, for every step I take to attain success in both will bring me nearer to you. How could anything now seem painful to me? Do not think so ill of me as to believe that, I implore you. What is a little toil, if it conquers so much happiness? Have I not a thousand times implored heaven to let me purchase it at the price of my blood? Oh! how happy I am! how happy I am going to be!

Adieu, my angel, my beloved Adèle! Adieu! I will kiss your hair and go to bed. Still I am far from you, but I can dream of you. Soon perhaps you will be at my side. Adieu; pardon the delirium of your husband who embraces you, and who adores you, both for this life and another.

Your picture?

OSCAR WILDE to LORD ALFRED DOUGLAS

[c. 1891]

My own dear boy – Your sonnet is quite lovely and it is a marvel that those red roseleaf lips of yours should be made no less for the music of song than for the madness of kissing. Your slim gilt soul walks between passion and poetry. I know that

Hyacinthus, whom Apollo loved so madly, was you in Greek days. Why are you alone in London, and when do you go to Salisbury? Do go there and cool your hands in the grey twilight of Gothic things, and come here whenever you like. It is a lovely place; it only lacks you, but go to Salisbury first. Always with undying love,

Yours,
Oscar.

Robert Schumann to Clara Wieck

[1838]
The 2nd.

How happy your last letters have made me – those since Christmas Eve! I should like to call you by all the endearing epithets, and yet I can find no lovelier word than the simple word 'dear,' but there is a particular way of saying it. My dear one, then, I have wept for joy to think that you are mine, and often wonder if I deserve you. One would think that no one man's heart and brain could stand all the things that are crowded into one day. Where do these thousands of thoughts, wishes, sorrows, joys and hopes, come from? Day in, day out, the procession goes on. But how light-hearted I was yesterday and the day before! There shone out of your letters so noble a spirit, such faith, such a wealth of love! What would I not do for love of you, my own Clara! The knights of old were better off; they could go through fire or slay dragons to win their ladies, but we of today have to content ourselves with more prosaic methods, such as smoking fewer cigars, and the like. After all, though, we can love, knights or no knights; and so, as ever, only the times change, not men's hearts.

I have a hundred things to write to you, great and small, if only

I could do it neatly, but my writing grows more and more indistinct, a sign, I fear, of heart weakness. There are terrible hours when your image forsakes me, when I wonder anxiously whether I have ordered my life as wisely as I might, whether I had any right to bind you to me, my angel, or can really make you as happy as I should wish. These doubts all arise, I am inclined to think, from your father's attitude towards me. It is so easy to accept other people's estimate of oneself. Your father's behaviour makes me ask myself if I am really so bad – of such humble standing – as to invite such treatment from anyone. Accustomed to easy victory over difficulties, to the smiles of fortune, and to affection, I have been spoiled by having things made too easy for me, and now I have to face refusal, insult and calumny. I have read of many such things in novels, but I thought too highly of myself to imagine I could ever be the hero of a family tragedy of the Kotzebue sort myself. If I had ever done your father an injury, he might well hate me; but I cannot see why he should despise me and, as you say, hate me without any reason. But my turn will come, and I will then show him how I love you and himself; for I will tell you, as a secret, that I really love and respect your father for his many great and fine qualities, as no one but yourself can do. I have a natural inborn devotion and reverence for him, as for all strong characters, and it makes his antipathy for me doubly painful. Well, he may some time declare peace, and say to us, 'Take each other, then.'

You cannot think how your letter has raised and strengthened me. . . . You are splendid, and I have much more reason to be proud of you than you of me. I have made up my mind, though, to read all your wishes in your face. Then you will think, even though you don't say it, that your Robert is a really good sort, that he is entirely yours, and loves you more than words can say. You shall indeed have cause to think so in the happy future. I still see you as you looked in your little cap that last evening. I still hear you call me *du*. Clara, I heard nothing of what you said but that *du*. Don't you remember?

But I see you in many another unforgettable guise. Once you

were in a black dress, going to the theatre with Emilia List; it was during our separation. I know you will not have forgotten; it is vivid with me. Another time you were walking in the Thomasgässchen with an umbrella up, and you avoided me in desperation. And yet another time, as you were putting on your hat after a concert, our eyes happened to meet, and yours were full of the old unchanging love. I picture you in all sorts of ways, as I have seen you since. I did not look at you much, but you charmed me so immeasurably. ... Ah, I can never praise you enough for yourself or for your love of me, which I don't really deserve.

Robert

FRANZ LISZT to MARIE D'AGOULT

Thursday morning [1834]

My heart overflows with emotion and joy! I do not know what heavenly languor, what infinite pleasure permeates it and burns me up. It is as if I had never loved!!! Tell me whence these uncanny disturbances spring, these inexpressible foretastes of delight, these divine tremors of love. Oh! all this can only spring from you, sister, angel, woman, Marie! ... All this can only be, is surely nothing less than a gentle ray streaming from your fiery soul, or else some secret poignant teardrop which you have long since left in my breast.

My God, my God, never force us apart, take pity on us! But what am I saying? Forgive my weakness, how couldst Thou divide us! Thou wouldst have nothing but pity for us ... No, no! ... It is not in vain that our flesh and our souls quicken and become immortal through Thy Word, which cries out deep within us Father, Father ... it is not in vain that Thou callest us, that Thou reachest out Thine hand to us, that our broken hearts seek their refuge in Thee. ... O! we thank, bless and praise Thee, O

God, for all that Thou hast given us, and all that Thou hast prepared for us. . . .

This is to be – to be!*

Marie! Marie!

Oh let me repeat that name a hundred times, a thousand times over; for three days now it has lived within me, oppressed me, set me afire. I am not writing to you, no, I am close beside you. I see you, I hear you. . . . Eternity in your arms. . . . Heaven, Hell, everything, all is within you, redoubled. . . . Oh! Leave me free to rave in my delirium. Drab, tame, constricting reality is no longer enough for me. We must live our lives to the full, loving and suffering to extremes! . . . Oh! you believe me capable of self-sacrifice, chastity, temperance and piety, do you not? But let no more be said of this . . . it is up to you to question, to draw conclusions, to save me as you see fit. Leave me free to rave in my delirium, since you can do nothing, nothing at all for me.

This is to be! to be!!!*

* These lines were in English in the original letter.

JANE WELSH CARLYLE to THOMAS CARLYLE

Templand,
30 December, 1828.

Goody, Goody, dear Goody, – you said you would weary and I do hope in my heart you are wearying. It will be so sweet to make it all up to you in kisses when I return. You will *take me* and hear all my bits of experiences, and your heart will beat when you find how I have longed to return to you. Darling, Dearest, Loveliest, 'The Lord bless you.' I think of you every hour, every moment. I love you and admire you like, – like anything. My own Good Good! But to get away on Sunday was not in my power my mother argued, entreated, and finally *grat*. I held out on the ground of having appointed Alick to meet me at Church; but that was untenable, John Kerr could be sent off at break of day to tell that I could not come. I urged that the household would find themselves destitute of every Christian *comfoart*, unless I were home before Wednesday. That could be taken care of by sending anything that was wanted from here. Tea, sugar, butcher's meat, everything was at my service. Well, but I wanted, I said, to be your *first foot* on New Year's Day. I might be gratified in this also. She would *hire a post-chaise and take me over for that day* on condition that I returned at night! In short, she had a remedy for everything but death, and I could not without seeming unkind and ungracious, refuse to stay longer than I proposed. So I write this letter 'with my own hand' that you may not be *disappointed* from day to day but prepare to welcome me in 'your choicest mood' on Sunday. If the day is at all tolerable, perhaps Alick or you will meet me at Church. Mrs. Crichton, of Dabton, was very pressing that you and I should spend some days with them just now, 'when their house was full of company'. But I assured her it would be losing labour to ask you. However, by way of consolation, I have agreed to 'refresh' a party for her with my presence on Friday, and held out some hope that you would visit them at your leisure. 'I am sure the kindness of those people. . . .' 'The Lord Bless them'!

Dearest, I wonder if you are getting any victual. There must be cocks at least, and the chickens will surely have laid their eggs. I have many an anxious thought about you; and I wonder if you sleep at nights, or if you are wandering about – on, on – smoking and killing mice. Oh, if I was there I could put my arms so close about your neck, hush you into the softest sleep you have had since I went away. Goodnight – you will get a parcel by Macnight and Andrew Watsons in which there is a little tea in case it be needed, for I do not expect the things from Ednr. this week as I understand Eliza is gone out of town for a few days to some great house-heating.

Good-night, my beloved. Dream of me.

I am ever,
Your own Goody.

[68]

Friday [12 December 1845]

For me, my dearest love, there are twenty-three sacred towns. They are these: Neuchâtel, Geneva, Vienna, St. Petersburg, Dresden, Cannstadt, Karlsruhe, Strasbourg, Passy, Fontainebleau, Orléans, Bourges, Tours, Blois, Paris, Rotterdam, the Hague, Antwerp, Brussels, Baden, Lyon, Toulon, Naples. I do not know what they mean to you but for me, when one of these names enters my thoughts, it is as if a Chopin were touching a piano key; the hammer awakens sounds which reverberate through my soul, and a complete poem takes shape.

Neuchâtel is like a white lily, pure, filled with pervasive scents; youth, freshness, excitement, hope, fleetingly perceived happiness. Geneva is the passion of dreams, the kind of dream where life is flashed before one, offered for ... oh! my God, I would have died of ecstasy had I been able to kiss your hand! And what an evening! What youth! I cannot think how you could fail to have kept that sodden piece of silk as I have kept the cloth with which I brushed away the fluff from a certain place on the floor which will be before my eyes when I die! ... Geneva is our zenith; our golden harvest! Vienna is mourning in the midst of joy. I came, certain of having nothing but sadness before me; Vienna, my purest act of devotion. And St. Petersburg? The blue salon of la Néva! the first initiation of my sweetheart, the first step in her education. What a union: it lasted for two months without a false note, unless one is to count that argument over the hat and the one about the expense of engaging a cook. The first moments of our unrestrained intercourse; the dawn of the marriage of our souls and the apprehensions of my precious pet fill these memories with delight, for I know that she will return to them to find reasons for loving more strongly, when she sees how unfair to her poor Noré her misconceptions were. Dresden is hunger and thirst, misery in the midst of happiness, a poor man casting himself on the richest of all feasts. Karlsruhe, the alms given to a pauper. But Strasbourg, oh! we are sure of love by now, it has the splendour of Louis XIV;

[69]

it holds the certain promise of mutual happiness. And Passy, Fontainebleau? Here is the genius of Beethoven; the sublime! Orléans, Bourges, Tours and Blois are concertos, well-loved symphonies, each of a more or less sunny character but tinged with sombre notes from my sweetheart's suffering. Paris, Rotterdam, the Hague, Antwerp are the last blooms of autumn. But Brussels is worthy of Cannstadt and of us. It is the triumph of two uniquely loving spirits. I think of it often and I feel us to be inexhaustible. Baden was the culmination; harmony for all eternity. There was there all the passion of Geneva, of that evening when I saw you again; and the combined desires of two mutually adoring hearts. But Lyon! oh! Lyon, showed me my love transcended by a charm, a tenderness, a perfect quality of caresses and a loving gentleness which makes Lyon for me one of those shibboleths special in a man's life, and which, when spoken, are like the holy word with which a man may open the path to heaven! Toulon is the daughter of Lyon, while all these riches were crowned by the delights of Naples, worthy of heaven, nature and these two sweethearts.

Such then are my flights of fancy when, weary of writing, I think of the rare perfection of her who was at birth so aptly named Eve, for she is unique on earth; there cannot be another so angelic, no other woman who could embody more gentleness, more ingenuity, more love, more inspiration in her caresses. Oh! all memories of Madame de B. are distant indeed! True love, the love of a young and beautiful woman, endowed with such charms, has nothing to fear. So, dearest heart, you are loved and your darling little treasure is kissed a hundred times a day in my thoughts. Guard it well. A thousand embraces to remind us of our twenty-three towns.

NATHANIEL HAWTHORNE to SOPHIA PEABODY

Boston, 17 April, 1839

My Dearest, – I feel pretty secure against intruders, for the bad weather will defend me from foreign invasion; and as to Cousin Haley, he and I had a bitter political dispute last evening, at the close of which he went to bed in high dudgeon, and probably will not speak to me these three days. Thus you perceive that strife and wrangling, as well as east-winds and rain, are the methods of a kind Providence to promote my comfort, – which would not have been so well secured in any other way. Six or seven hours of cheerful solitude! But I will not be alone. I invite your spirit to be with me, – at any hour and as many hours as you please, – but especially at the twilight hour, before I light my lamp. I bid you at that particular time, because I can see visions more vividly in the dusky glow of firelight than either by daylight or lamplight. Come, and let me renew my spell against headache and other direful effects of the east-wind. How I wish I could give you a portion of my insensibility! and yet I should be almost afraid of some radical transformation, were I to produce a change in that respect. If you cannot grow plump and rosy and tough and vigorous without being changed into another nature, then I do think, for this short life, you had better remain just what you are. Yes; but you will be the same to me, because we have met in Eternity, and there our intimacy was formed. So get well as soon as you possibly can, and I shall never doubt that you are the same Sophie who have so often leaned upon my arm and needed its superfluous strength. I never, till now, had a friend who could give me repose; all have disturbed me, and, whether for pleasure or pain, it was still disturbance. But peace overflows from your heart into mine. Then I feel that there is a Now, and that Now must be always calm and happy, and that sorrow and evil are but phantoms that seem to flit across it . . .

When this week's first letter came, I held it a long time in my hand, marvelling at the superscription. How did you contrive to write it? Several times since I have pored over it, to discover how much of yourself mingled with my share of it; and certainly there is grace flung over the fac-simile, which never was seen in my harsh, uncouth autograph, and yet none of the strength is lost. You are wonderful.

What a beautiful day! and I had a double enjoyment of it – for your sake and my own. I have been to walk, this afternoon, to Bunker's Hill and the Navy Yard, and am tired, because I had not your arm to support me.

God keep you from east-winds and every other evil.

Your own friend,

N.H.

Nathaniel Hawthorne to Sophia Peabody

[c. 1839]

5 December

Dearest, – I wish I had the gift of making rhymes, for methinks there is poetry in my head and heart since I have been in love with you. You are a Poem. Of what sort, then? Epic? Mercy on me, no! A sonnet? No; for that is too labored and artificial. You are a sort of sweet, simple, gay, pathetic ballad, which Nature is singing, sometimes with tears, sometimes with smiles, and sometimes with intermingled smiles and tears.

Sophia Peabody to Nathaniel Hawthorne

31 December, 1839

Best Beloved, – I send you some allumettes wherewith to kindle the taper. There are very few but my second finger could no longer perform extra duty. These will serve till the wounded one be healed, however. How beautiful is it to provide even this slightest convenience for you, dearest! I cannot tell you how much I love you, in this back-handed style. My love is not in this attitude, – it rather bends forward to meet you.

What a year has this been to us! My definition of Beauty is, that it is love, and therefore includes both truth and good. But those only who love as we do can feel the significance and force of this.

My ideas will not flow in these crooked strokes. God be with you. I am very well, and have walked far in Danvers this cold morning. I am full of the glory of the day. God bless you this night of the old year. It has proved the year of our nativity. Has not the old earth passed away from us? – are not all things new?

Your Sophie

PASSIONS

JOHN KEATS to FANNY BRAWNE

[March 1820?]

Sweetest Fanny,

You fear, sometimes, I do not love you so much as you wish? My dear Girl I love you ever and ever and without reserve. The more I have known you the more have I lov'd. In every way – even my jealousies have been agonies of Love, in the hottest fit I ever had I would have died for you. I have vex'd you too much. But for Love! Can I help it? You are always new. The last of your kisses was ever the sweetest; the last smile the brightest; the last movement the gracefullest. When you pass'd my window home yesterday, I was fill'd with as much admiration as if I had then seen you for the first time. You uttered a half complaint once that I only lov'd your Beauty. Have I nothing else then to love in you but that? Do not I see a heart naturally furnish'd with wings imprison itself with me? No ill prospect has been able to turn your thoughts a moment from me. This perhaps should be as much a subject of sorrow as joy – but I will not talk of that. Even if you did not love me I could not help an entire devotion to you: how much more deeply then must I feel for you knowing you love me. My Mind has been the most discontented and restless one that ever was put into a body too small for it. I never felt my Mind repose upon anything with complete and undistracted enjoyment – upon no person but you. When you are in the room my thoughts never fly out of window: you always concentrate my whole senses. The anxiety shown about our Loves in your last note is an immense pleasure to me: however you must not suffer such speculations to molest you any more: nor will I any more believe you can have the least pique against me. Brown is gone out – but here is Mrs Wylie – when she is gone I shall be awake for you. – Remembrances to your Mother.

Your affectionate

J. Keats

JULIE DE LESPINASSE to HIPPOLYTE DE GUIBERT

13 November, 1774

Ah, my friend, you hurt me, and a great curse for you and for me is the feeling which animates me. You were right in saying that you did not need to be loved as I know how to love; no, that is not your measure; you are so perfectly lovable, that you must be or become the first object (of desire) of all these charming ladies, who stick upon their heads all they had in it, and who are so lovable that they love themselves by preference above everything. You will give pleasure, you will satisfy the vanity of nearly all women. By what fatality have you held me to life, and you make me die of anxiety and of pain? My friend, I do not complain; but it distresses me that you pay no heed to my repose; this thought chills and tears my heart alternately. How can one have an instant's tranquillity with a man whose head is as defective as his coach, who counts for nothing the dangers, who never foresees anything, who is incapable of taking care, of exactitude, to whom it never happens to do what he has projected; in a word, a man whom everything attracts, and whom nothing can stay nor give stability. ... Good night. My door has not been opened once to-day, but what my heart palpitated. There were moments when I feared to hear your voice, and then I was disconsolate that it was not your voice. So many contradictions, so many contrary movements are true, and can be explained in three words: *I love you.*

NAPOLEON BONAPARTE to JOSEPHINE DE BEAUHARNAIS

Paris, December 1795

I wake filled with thoughts of you. Your portrait and the intoxicating evening which we spent yesterday have left my senses in turmoil. Sweet, incomparable Josephine, what a strange effect you have on my heart! Are you angry? Do I see you looking sad? Are you worried? . . . My soul aches with sorrow, and there can be no rest for your lover; but is there still more in store for me when, yielding to the profound feelings which overwhelm me, I draw from your lips, from your heart a love which consumes me with fire? Ah! it was last night that I fully realised how false an image of you your portrait gives!

You are leaving at noon; I shall see you in three hours.

Until then, mio dolce amor, a thousand kisses; but give me none in return, for they set my blood on fire.

NAPOLEON BONAPARTE to JOSEPHINE BONAPARTE

To citizen Bonaparte,
care of citizen Beauharnais,
6, rue Chantereine,
Paris.

Nice, 10 Germinal, year IV [1796]

I have not spent a day without loving you; I have not spent a night without embracing you; I have not so much as drunk a single cup of tea without cursing the pride and ambition which force me to remain separated from the moving spirit of my life. In the midst of my duties, whether I am at the head of my army or inspecting the camps, my beloved Josephine stands alone in my heart, occupies my mind, fills my thoughts. If I am moving away from you with the speed of the Rhône torrent, it is only that I may see you again more quickly. If I rise to work in the middle of the night, it is because this may hasten by a matter of days the arrival of my sweet love. Yet in your letter of the 23rd. and 26th. Ventôse, you call me *vous. Vous* yourself! Ah! wretch, how could you have written this letter? How cold it is! And then there are those four days between the 23rd. and the 26th.; what were you doing that you failed to write to your husband?... Ah, my love, that *vous,* those four days make me long for my former indifference. Woe to the person responsible! May he, as punishment and penalty, experience what my convictions and the evidence (which is in your friend's favour) would make me experience! Hell has no torments great enough! Nor do the Furies have serpents enough! *Vous! Vous!* Ah! how will things stand in two weeks?... My spirit is heavy; my heart is fettered and I am terrified by my fantasies. ... You love me less; but you will get over the loss. One day you will love me no longer; at least tell me; then I shall know how I have come to deserve this misfortune. ... Farewell, my wife: the torment, joy, hope and moving spirit of my life; whom I love, whom I fear, who fills me with tender feelings which draw me close to Nature, and with violent impulses as tumultuous as thunder. I ask of you neither eternal love, nor fidelity, but simply ... *truth,* unlimited honesty. The day when you say 'I love you less', will mark the end of my love and the last day of my life. If my heart were base enough to love without being loved in return I would tear it to pieces. Josephine! Josephine! Remember what I have sometimes said to you: Nature has endowed me with a virile and decisive character. It has built yours out of lace and gossamer. Have you ceased to love me? Forgive me, love of my life, my soul is racked by conflicting forces.

My heart, obsessed by you, is full of fears which prostrate me with misery. ... I am distressed not to be calling you by name. I shall wait for you to write it.

Farewell! Ah! if you love me less you can never have loved me. In that case I shall truly be pitiable.

Bonaparte

P.S. – The war this year has changed beyond recognition. I have had meat, bread and fodder distributed; my armed cavalry will soon be on the march. My soldiers are showing inexpressible confidence in me; you alone are a source of chagrin to me; you alone are the joy and torment of my life. I send a kiss to your children, whom you do not mention. By God! If you did, your letters would be half as long again. Then visitors at ten o'clock in the morning would not have the pleasure of seeing you. Woman!!!

JULIETTE DROUET to VICTOR HUGO

[1833]

To my beloved,

I have left you, my beloved. May the memory of my love follow and comfort you during our separation. If you only knew how much I love you, how essential you are to my life, you would not dare to stay away for an instant, you would always remain by my side, your heart pressed close to my heart, your soul to my soul.

It is now eleven o'clock in the evening. I have not seen you. I am waiting for you with great impatience, as I will wait for you always. It seems a whole century since I last saw you, since I last looked upon your features and became intoxicated with your gaze. Given my ill-luck, I shall probably not see you tonight.

Oh! come back, my love, my life, come back.

If you knew how I long for you, how the memory of last night leaves me delirious with joy and full of desire. How I long to give myself up in ecstasy to your sweet breath and to those kisses from your lips which fill me with delight!

My Victor, forgive me all my extravagances. They are a further token of my love. Love me. I need your love as a touchstone of my existence. It is the sun which breathes life into me.

I am going to bed. I shall fall asleep praying of you. My need to see you happy gives me faith.

My last waking thoughts, and all my dreams, are of you.

Juliette

KING JAMES I to GEORGE VILLIERS, FIRST DUKE OF BUCKINGHAM

[c. 1622]

My only sweet and dear child,

I am now so miserable a coward, as I do nothing but weep and mourn; for I protest to God, I rode this afternoon a great way in the park without speaking to anybody, and the tears trickling down my cheeks, as now they do, that I can scarcely see to write. But, alas! what shall I do at our parting? The only small comfort that I can have will be to pry into thy defects with the eye of an enemy, and of every mote to make a mountain; and so harden my heart against thy absence. But this little malice is like jealousy, proceeding from a sweet root; but in one point it overcometh it, for, as it proceeds from love, so it cannot but end in love.

Sweet heart! be earnest with Kate to come and meet thee at New Hall within eight or ten days after this. Cast thee to be here tomorrow, as near as about two in the afternoon as thou canst, and come galloping hither. Remember thy picture, and suffer none of the Council to come here – for God's sake! Write not a word again, and let no creature see this letter. The Lord of heaven and earth bless thee, and my sweet daughter, and my sweet little grandchild, and all thy blessed family, and send thee a happier return – both now and thou knowest when – to thy dear dad and Christian gossip.

James R.

LORD BYRON to LADY CAROLINE LAMB

[August 1812?]

My dearest Caroline,

If tears which you saw and know I am not apt to shed, – if the agitation in which I parted from you, – agitation which you must have perceived through the *whole* of this most *nervous* affair, did not commence until the moment of leaving you approached, – if all I have said and done, and am still but too ready to say and do, have not sufficiently proved what my real feelings are, and must ever be towards you, my love, I have no other proof to offer. God knows, I wish you happy, and when I quit you, or rather you, from a sense of duty to your husband and mother, quit me, you shall acknowledge the truth of what I again promise and vow, that no other in word or deed, shall ever hold the place in my affections, which is, and shall be, most sacred to you, till I am nothing. I never knew till *that moment* the *madness* of my dearest and most beloved friend; I cannot express myself; this is no time for words, but I shall have a pride, a melancholy pleasure, in suffering what you yourself can scarcely conceive, for you do not know me. I am about to go out with a heavy heart, because my appearing this evening will stop any absurd story which the event of the day might give rise to. Do you think *now* I am *cold* and *stern* and *artful*? Will even *others* think so? Will your *mother* ever – that mother to whom we must indeed sacrifice much, more, much more on my part than she shall ever know or can imagine? 'Promise not to love you!' ah, Caroline, it is past promising. But I shall attribute all concessions to the proper motive, and never cease to feel all that you have already witnessed, and more than can ever be known but to my own heart, – perhaps to yours. May God protect, forgive, and bless you. Ever, and even more than ever,

Your most attached,

Byron

P.S. – These taunts which have driven you to this, my dearest Caroline, were it not for your mother and the kindness of your connections, is there anything on earth or heaven that would have made me so happy as to have made you mine long ago? and not less *now* than *then*, but *more* than ever at this time. You know I would with pleasure give up all here and all beyond the grave for you, and in refraining from this, must my motives be misunderstood? I care not who knows this, what use is made of it, – it is to

[83]

you and to *you* only that they are *yourself* [*sic*]. I was and am yours freely and most entirely, to obey, to honour, love – and fly with you when, where, and how you yourself *might* and *may* determine.

LORD BYRON to TERESA GUICCIOLI

Bologna, 25 August, 1819.

My dearest Teresa,

I have read this book in your garden; – my love, you were absent, or else I could not have read it. It is a favourite book of yours, and the writer was a friend of mine. You will not understand these English words, and *others* will not understand them, – which is the reason I have not scrawled them in Italian. But you will recognize the handwriting of him who passionately loved you, and you will divine that, over a book which was yours, he could only think of love.

In that word, beautiful in all languages, but most so in yours – *Amor mio* – is comprised my existence here and hereafter. I feel I exist here, and I feel I shall exist hereafter, – to *what* purpose you will decide; my destiny rests with you, and you are a woman, eighteen years of age, and two out of a convent, I wish that you had staid there, with all my heart, – or, at least, that I had never met you in your married state.

But all this is too late. I love you, and you love me,– at least, you *say so*, and *act* as if you *did so*, which last is a great consolation in all events. But *I* more than love you, and cannot cease to love you.

Think of me, sometimes, when the Alps and ocean divide us, – but they never will, unless you *wish* it.

Byron

[84]

JEALOUSIES

IDA JOHN to DORELIA (DOROTHY MCNEILL)

[1905]

. . . I tried not to be horrid – I know I am – I never hardly feel generous now like I did at first – I suppose you feel this through everything – I tried to be jolly – it is easy to be superficially jolly – I hate to think I made you miserable but I know I have – Gus blames me entirely for *everything* now – I daresay he's right – but when I think of some things I feel I suffered too much – it was like physical suffering it was so intense – like being burnt or something – I can't feel I am entirely responsible for this horrid ending – it was nature that was the enemy to our scheme. I have often wondered you have not gone away before – it has always been open to you to go, and if you have been as unhappy as Gus says you should have told me. I do not think it likely Gus and I can live together after this – I want to separate – I feel sick at heart. At present I hate you generally but I don't know if I really do. It is all impossible now and we are simply living in a convention you know – a way of talking to each other which has no depth or heart. I should like to know if it gives you a feeling of relief and flying away to freedom to think of going . . . I don't care what Gus thinks of me now, of course he'd be wild at this letter. He seems centuries away. He puts himself away. I think he's a mean and childish creature besides being the fine old chap he is.

I came here in order to have the rest cure, and I am, but it makes things seem worse than if one is occupied – but of course it will all come all right in the end. I know you and Gus think I ought to think of you as the sufferer, but I can't. You are free – the man you love at present, loves you – you don't care for convention or what people think – of course your future is perilous, but you love it. You are a wanderer – you would hate safety and cages – why are you to be pitied? It is only the ones who are bound who are to be pitied – the slaves. It seems to me utterly misjudging the case to pity you. You are living your life – you chose it – you did it because you wanted to – didn't you? Do you regret it? I thought you were a wild free bird who loved life in its glorious hardships. If I am to think of you as a sad female who needs protection I must indeed change my ideas – and yet Gus seems to think it is all your sorrow. I do not understand. It was for your freedom and all you represented I envied you so. Because you meant to Gus all that lay outside the dull home, the unspeakable fireside, the gruesome dinner table – that I became so hopeless – I was the chain – you were the key to unlock it. This is what I have been made to feel ever since you came. Gus will deny it but he denies many facts which are daily occurrences – apparently denies them because they are true and he wants to pretend they aren't. One feels what is, doesn't one? Nothing can change this fact – that you are the one outside who calls a man to *apparent* freedom and wild rocks and wind and air – and I am the one inside who says come to dinner, and whom to live with is apparent slavery. Neither Gus nor I are strong enough to find freedom in domesticity – though I know it is there.

You are the wild bird – fly away – as Gus says our life does not suit you. He will follow, never fear. There was never a poet could stay at home. Do not think I consider myself to be pitied either. I shudder when I think of those times, simply because it was pain. ... It has robbed me of the tenderness I felt for you – but you can do without that – and I would do anything for you if you would ever ask me to – you still seem to belong to us.

I.

Vienna, April 29th, 1782

Dearest, Most Beloved Friend!

Surely you will still allow me to address you by this name? Surely you do not hate me so much that I may be your friend no longer, and you – no longer mine? And even if you will not be my friend any longer, yet you cannot forbid me to wish you well, my friend, since it has become very natural for me to do so. Do think over what you said to me to-day. In spite of all my entreaties you have thrown me over three times and told me to my face that you intend to have nothing more to do with me. I (to whom it means more than it does to you to lose the object of my love) am not so hot-tempered, so rash and so senseless as to accept my dismissal. I love you far too well to do so. I entreat you, therefore, to ponder and reflect upon the cause of all this unpleasantness, which arose from my being annoyed that you were so impudently inconsiderate as to say to your sisters – and, be it noted, in my presence – that you had let a *chapeau* measure the calves of your legs. No woman who cares for her honour can do such a thing. It is quite a good maxim to do as one's company does. At the same time there are many other factors to be considered – as, for example, whether only intimate friends and acquaintances are present – whether I am a child or a *marriageable* girl – more particularly, whether I am already betrothed – but, above all, whether only people of my own social standing or my social inferiors – or, what is even more important, my social superiors are in the company? If it be true that the Baroness herself allowed it to be done to her, the case is still quite different, for she is already past her prime and cannot possibly attract any longer – and besides, she is inclined to be promiscuous with her favours. I hope, dearest friend, that, even if you do not wish to become my wife, you will never lead a life like hers. If it was quite impossible for you to resist the desire to take part in the game (although it is not always wise for a man to do so, and still less for a woman), then why in the name of Heaven did you not take the ribbon and measure your own calves *yourself* (as *all self-respecting women* have done on similar occasions in my presence) and not allow a *chapeau* to do so? – Why, I myself *in the presence of others* would never have done such a thing to you. I should have handed you the ribbon myself. Still less, then, should you have allowed it to be done to you by a stranger – a man about whom I know nothing. But it is all over now; and the least acknowledgement of your somewhat thoughtless behaviour on that occasion would have made everything all right again; and if you will not make a grievance of it, dearest friend, everything will still be all right. You realise now how much I love you. *I do not fly into a passion as you do.* I think, I reflect and I feel. *If you will but surrender to your feelings,* then I know that this very day I shall be able to say with absolute confidence that Constanze is the virtuous, honourable, prudent and loyal sweetheart of her honest and devoted

Mozart

NADEJDA VON MECK to PIOTR TCHAIKOVSKY

Brailov

Sept. 26, 1879

Friday at 8 A.M.

How sorry I am, my dearest, that you feel so badly in Petersburg, but – forgive me – I am glad you are homesick for Brailov. I doubt if you could ever understand how jealous I am of you, in spite of the absence of personal contact between us. Do you know that I am jealous in the most unpardonable way, as a woman is jealous of the man she loves? Do you know that when you married it was terribly hard for me, as though something had broken in my heart? The thought that you were near that woman was bitter and unbearable.

And do you know what a wicked person I am? I rejoiced when you were unhappy with her! I reproached myself for that feeling.

I don't think I betrayed myself in any way, and yet I could not destroy my feelings. They are something a person does not order.

I hated that woman because she did not make you happy, but I would have hated her a hundred times more if you had been happy with her. I thought she had robbed me of what should be mine only, what is my right, because I love you more than anyone and value you above everything in the world.

If this knowledge bothers you, forgive my involuntary confession. I have spoken out. The reason is, the symphony. But I believe it is better for you to know that I am not such an idealistic person as you think. And then, it cannot change anything in our relationship. I don't want any change. I should like to be sure that nothing will be changed as my life draws to its close, that nobody. . . . But that I have no right to say. Forgive me and forget all I have said – my mind is upset.

Forgive me, please, and realize that I feel well and that I am in need of nothing. Good-bye, dear friend; forget this letter, but do not forget your heartily loving,

N. von Meck

P.S.   Would you mind, please, acknowledging the receipt of this letter?

ELLEN TERRY to GEORGE BERNARD SHAW

[October 1896]

Darling, I've not read your letter, but I must tell you I dislike folk who are not reserved, and will tell me of your *Janets* and things and make me mad, when I *only* want to know whether they think you would if we met, have a horrible dislike of me when you found me such an old thing, and so different to the Ellen you've seen on the stage. I'm so pale when I'm off the stage, and rouge becomes me, and I know I shall have to take to it if I consent to let you see me. And it would be so pathetic, for not even the rouge would make you admire me away from the stage. Oh what a curse it is to be an actress! . . .

I can't compete 'cos I'm not pretty.

ZELDA FITZGERALD to F. SCOTT FITZGERALD

[c. 1919]

Scott, you're really awfully silly – In the first place, I haven't kissed anybody good-bye, and in the second place, nobody's left in the first place – You know, darling, that I love you too much to want to. If I did have an honest – or dishonest – desire to kiss just one or two people, I *might* – but I couldn't ever want to – my mouth is yours.

But s'pose I did – Don't you know it'd just be absolutely *nothing* – Why can't you understand that nothing means anything except your darling self and your love – I wish we'd hurry and I'd be yours so you'd *know* – Sometimes I almost despair of making you feel sure – so sure that nothing could ever make you doubt like I do –

JOHN RUSKIN to EFFIE GRAY

Denmark Hill
9 November 1847

My own Effie – my kind Effie – my mistress – my friend – my queen – my darling – my only love – how good of you – and I can't answer you a word today. I am going into town with my mother in half an hour – and have all manner of things to do, first – but I am

so glad that you have my letter speaking about this very thing –
Indeed I *never* will be jealous of you – and I will keep that
purer form of jealousy – that longing for more love – within
proper limits – and you will soon find out how to manage this
weakness – and perhaps to conquer it altogether; I can't enter into
details today – but indeed it was anxiety and weakness of nerve
which made me so fretful when you were here – natural enough I
think – and even then, I was only jealous of *some people* – and that
because I was hurt by your *condescension* – it was, I think – at the
root – more pride than jealousy – I was speaking of large parties to
my mother yesterday for you – she said 'You wouldn't like to see
her surrounded by a circle of gentlemen like Mrs Loddell?'
'Indeed I should,' I said.

Effie Gray to John Ruskin

Bowerswell
8 February 1848

I told Papa the other day that you said you never would be really
jealous without cause and he says unfortunately jealous people
always *find cause* which I think quite true but I hope at heart you
are really not a jealous being, and the absurdity of your giving as a
reason that my manner to you and other people was quite the
same is really the most preposterous thing I ever heard. You must
have been thinking of something else when you wrote that! but
really John I love you so much that I don't think much about *the*
jealous part of you for I do not believe you will be at all so after we
are married and I daresay you will allow me to ask anybody I like
to take some pudding without behaving afterwards as madly as
Mr. Munn.

BENJAMIN FRANKLIN to MADAME BRILLON

[10 November 1779]

What a difference, my dear friend, between you and me! You find innumerable faults in me, whereas I see only one fault in you (but perhaps it is the fault of my glasses). I mean this kind of avarice which leads you to seek a monopoly on all my affections, and not to allow me any for the agreeable ladies of your country. Do you imagine that it is impossible for my affection (or my tenderness) to be divided without being diminished? You deceive yourself, and you forget the playful manner with which you stopped me. You renounce and totally exclude all that might be of the flesh in our affection, allowing me only some kisses, civil and honest, such as you might grant your little cousins. What am I receiving that is so special as to prevent me from giving the same to others, without taking from what belongs to you? ... The sweet sounds brought forth from the pianoforte by your clever hands can be enjoyed by twenty people simultaneously without diminishing at all the pleasure you so obligingly mean for me, and I could, with as little reason, demand from your affection that no other ears but mine be allowed to be charmed by those sweet sounds.

JOHN KEATS to FANNY BRAWNE

[5 July 1820]
Wednesday Morng.

My dearest Girl,

I have been a walk this morning with a book in my hand, but as usual I have been occupied with nothing but you I wish I could say in an agreeable manner. I am tormented day and night. They talk of my going to Italy. 'Tis certain I shall never recover if I am to be so long separate from you yet with all this devotion to you I cannot persuade myself into any confidence of you. Past experience connected with the fact of my long separation from you gives me agonies which are scarcely to be talked of. When your mother comes I shall be very sudden and expert in asking her whether you have been to Mrs Dilke's, for she might say no to make me easy. I am literally worn to death, which seems my only recourse. I cannot forget what has pass'd. What? nothing with a man of the world, but to me deathful. I will get rid of this as much as possible. When you were in the habit of flirting with Brown you would have left off, could your own heart have felt one half of one pang mine did. Brown is a good sort of Man – he did not know he was doing me to death by inches. I feel the effect of every one of those hours in my side now; and for that cause, though he has done me many services, though I know his love and friendship for me, though at this moment I should be without pence were it not for his assistance, I will never see or speak to him until we are both old men, if we are to be. I *will* resent my heart having been made a football. You will call this madness. I have heard you say that it was not unpleasant to wait a few years – you have amusements – your mind is away – you have not brooded over one idea as I have, and how should you? You are to me an object intensely desireable – the air I breathe in a room empty of you is unhealthy. I am not the same to you – no – you can wait – you have a thousand activities – you can be happy without me. Any party, any thing to fill up the day has been enough. How have you pass'd this month? Who have you smil'd with? All this may seem savage in me. You do not feel as I do – you do not know what it is to love – one day you may – your time is not come. Ask yourself how many unhappy hours Keats has caused you in Loneliness. For myself I have been a Martyr the whole time, and for this reason I speak; the confession is forc'd from me by the torture. I appeal to you by the blood of that Christ you believe in: Do not write to me if you have done anything this month which it would have pained me to have seen. You may have altered – if you have not – if you still behave in dancing rooms and other societies as I have seen you – I do not want to live – if you have done so I wish this coming night

[95]

may be my last. I cannot live without you, and not only you but *chaste you; virtuous you.* The Sun rises and sets, the day passes, and you follow the bent of your inclination to a certain extent – you have no conception of the quantity of miserable feeling that passes through me in a day. – Be serious! Love is not a plaything – and again do not write unless you can do it with a crystal conscience. I would sooner die for want of you than—

Yours for ever

J. Keats

GALLANTRIES

Christ Church, Oxford,
28 October, 1876

My Dearest Gertrude:

You will be sorry, and surprised, and puzzled, to hear what a queer illness I have had ever since you went. I sent for the doctor, and said, 'Give me some medicine, for I'm tired.' He said, 'Nonsense and stuff! You don't want medicine: go to bed!' I said, 'No; it isn't the sort of tiredness that wants bed. I'm tired in the *face.*' He looked a little grave, and said, 'Oh, it's your *nose* that's tired: a person often talks too much when he thinks he nose a great deal.' I said, 'No, it isn't the nose. Perhaps it's the *hair.*' Then he looked rather grave, and said, '*Now* I understand: you've been playing too many hairs on the pianoforte.' No, indeed I haven't!' I said, and it isn't exactly the *hair*: it's more about the nose and chin.' Then he looked a good deal graver, and said, 'Have you been walking much on your chin lately?' I said, 'No.' 'Well!' he said, 'it puzzles me very much. Do you think that it's in the lips?' 'Of course!' I said. 'That's exactly what it is!'

Then he looked very grave indeed, and said, 'I think you must have been giving too many kisses.' 'Well,' I said, 'I did give one kiss to a baby child, a little friend of mine.' 'Think again,' he said; 'are you sure it was only one?' I thought again, and said, 'Perhaps it was eleven times.' Then the doctor said, 'You must not give her any more till your lips are quite rested again.' 'But what am I to do?' I said, 'because you see, I owe her a hundred and eighty-two more.' Then he looked so grave that the tears ran down his cheeks, and he said, 'You may send them to her in a box.' Then I remembered a little box that I once bought at Dover, and thought I would some day give it to *some* little girl or other. So I have packed them all in it very carefully. Tell me if they come safe, or if any are lost on the way.

MARCEL PROUST to LOUISA DE MORNAND

[1904?]
Thursday

Chère amie,

Your souvenir is precious to me, thank you for it. How I should love to walk with you in the streets of Blois, which must be a charming frame for your beauty. It is an old frame, a Renaissance frame. But it is a new frame, too, since I have never seen you in it. And in new places the people we love appear to us somehow new, too. I should find your beautiful eyes reflecting the lightness of a Touraine sky, your exquisite figure, outlined against the background of the old château, more moving than seeing you in just another dress; it would be like seeing you in a whole new costume. And I should like to see the effect of the pretty embroidery of one of the blue or pink dresses you wear so well, against the delicate stone embroideries worn by the old château with a grace which, even if a little ancient, is to my mind, none the less becoming. The pen with which I am writing you all this is so bad it will only write wrong-side up. My brain is a little that way, too. So don't be surprised if the result isn't brilliant. Besides, I only know how to tell women I admire and love them when I feel neither one nor the other. And you – you know that I admire you very much and love you very much. So I shall always express it to you very inadequately. Don't think that all this is an indiscreet, pretentious, and awkward way of trying to flirt with you. Not that this is of any importance, because if it were, you would have

[100]

sent me quickly on my way. I should rather die than make advances to a woman who is adored by a friend whose noble and sensitive heart endears him to me more each day. At least a small amount of friendship and a great deal of admiration may be permitted me. ... You will decide how you want it. While awaiting the verdict, risking all to win all, and with a boldness that is perhaps a result of the great distance between the rue de Courcelles and the chaussée de Saint-V ..., I am going to do something (while mentally asking A ...'s permission) that will bring me mad happiness if it is realized other than in just a letter. I embrace you tenderly, my dear Louisa.

Marcel Proust

If, as I hope for his sake and for yours (for the hours that you spend apart seem to me long, indeed, when I think of your sadness as well as his), A ... has returned to you, tell him chiefly please not to call me 'Proust' any more and, incidentally, that I like him very much. I send my respects to your sister, whom I don't know, but who must indeed be charming if she resembles you. If she combines your gentleness and your loyalty (which I appreciate most in you and which, if I am not mistaken, the future alone will fully reveal), she must be an accomplished person. But I suspect that I prefer you, nevertheless!

MARCEL PROUST to LAURE HAYMAN

[Summer 1892]
This Wednesday morning

Chère amie, chères délices,

Here are fifteen chrysanthemums, twelve for your twelve when they are faded, three to round out your twelve; I hope the stems will be extremely long as I requested. And that these flowers – proud and sad, like you, proud of being beautiful, and sad that everything is so stupid – will please you. Thank you again (and if I had not had examinations Saturday, I should have come to tell you so) for your kind thought of me. It would have amused me so to go to this eighteenth-century fête, to see these young men, who you say are clever and charming, united in their love of you. How well I understand them! It is only natural that a woman who is desirable and nothing more, the mere object of lust, should exasperate her lovers, set them one against the other. But when, like a work of art, a woman reveals the utmost refinement of charm, the most subtle grace, the most divine beauty, the most voluptuous intelligence, a common admiration for her is bound to unite, to establish a brotherhood. Co-religionists are made in Laure Hayman's name. And since she is a very special divinity, since her charm is not accessible to everyone, since one must have very subtle tastes in order to understand it, like an initiation of the mind and the senses, it is only right that the faithful should love each other, that among the initiates there should be understanding. So your whatnot of Saxe figures [an altar] seems to me one of the most charming things to be seen anywhere, and bound to be the rarest in existence since the days of Cleopatra and Aspasia. Therefore, I propose to call the present century the century of Laure Hayman and the ruling dynasty the Saxon line. – Forgive all this nonsense and allow me, when my examination is over, to bring you my tender respects.

Marcel Proust

P.S. On thinking it over, I should be rather embarrassed at becoming part of your collection of Saxe figures. If it is all right with you, I should rather see the one I most want to meet while he is calling on you. In that way if any of them find me tiresome, they will at least not find me indiscreet. And I shall not have to fear the vengeance of dukes or counts for having disturbed the collection.

THOMAS JEFFERSON to MARIA COSWAY

Paris Sep. 26. 1788.

Your favor of Aug. the 19., my very dear friend, is put into my hands this 26th. day of September 1788. and I answer it in the same instant to shew you there is nothing nearer my heart than to meet all the testimonies of your esteem. It is a strong one that you will occupy yourself for me on such a trifle as a visiting card. But sketch it only with your pencil, my friend, and do not make of it a serious business. This would render me uneasy, because I did not mean such a trespass on your time. A few strokes of your pencil on a card will be enjoiment enough for me.

I am going to America, and you to Italy. The one or the other of us goes the wrong way, for the way will ever be wrong which leads us farther apart. Mine is a journey of duty and of affection. I must deposit my daughters in the bosom of their friends and country. This done, I shall return to my station. My absence may be as short as five months, and certainly not longer than nine. How long my subsequent stay here may be I cannot tell. It would certainly be the longer had I a single friend here like yourself. – In going to Italy, be sure to cross the Alps at the Col de Tende. It is the best pass, because you need never get out of your carriage. It is practicable in seasons when all the other passes are shut up by snow. The roads leading to and from it are as fine as can possibly be, and you will see the castle of Saorgio. Take a good day for that part of your journey, and when you shall have sketched it in your portefeuille, and copied it more at leisure for yourself, tear out the leaf and send it to me. But why go to Italy? You have seen it, all the world has seen it, and ransacked it thousands of times. Rather join our good friend Mrs. Church in her trip to America. There you will find original scenes, scenes worthy of your pencil, such as the Natural bridge or the Falls of Niagara. Or participate with Trumbull the historical events of that country. These will have the double merit of being new, and of coming from you. I should find excuses for being sometimes of your parties. Think of this, my dear friend, mature the project with Mrs. Church, and let us all embark together at Havre. Adieu ma tres chere et excellente amie. Your's affectionately,

Th: J.

WALTER BAGEHOT to ELIZABETH WILSON

Herd's Hill,
22 November, 1857

My dearest Eliza,

I fear you will think the answer I wrote yesterday to your most kind and *delicious* letter, was very superficial, but I wrote it at once while people were talking and bothering me. I have now read yours over and over more times than I should like to admit. I awoke in the middle of the night and immediately lit a candle to read it a few times again. It has given me more pleasure than I ever received from a letter, and infinitely more than I thought it possible I could receive from one. I fancy that it is not now an effort to you to write to me – at least it reads as if it was written without effort. Yet it tells me things which with your deep and reserved nature it must have cost you much to put on paper. I wish indeed I could feel worthy of your affection – my reason, if not my imagination, is getting to believe you when you whisper to me that I have it, but as somebody says in Miss Austen, 'I do not at all mind having what is too good for me'; my delight is at times intense. You must not suppose because I tell you of the wild, burning pain which I have felt, and at times, though I am and *ought* to be much soothed, still feel, that my love for you has ever been mere suffering. Even at the worst there was a wild, delicious excitement which I would not have lost for the world. At first, and before the feeling was very great it was simple pleasure to me to come to Claverton, and the charm of our early intellectual talks was very great, although of late, and particularly since the day in the conservatory, the feeling has been too eager not to have a good deal of pain in it, and the tension of mind has really been very great at times, still the time that I have known and loved you is immensely the happiest I have ever known. My spirits always make me cheerful in a superficial way, but they do not *satisfy*, and somehow life even before I was engaged to you was sweeter and gentler, and the jars and jangles of action lost their influence, and literature had a new value since *you* liked my writing, and everything has had a gloss upon it. Though I have come to Claverton the last few times with the notion that the gloss would go – that I should burst out and you would be tranquil and kind and considerate and *refuse* and I should never see you again. I had a vision of the thing which I keep by me. As it has *not* happened I am afraid this is egotistical – indeed I know it is – but I am not sure that egotism is bad in letters, and if I write to you I *must* write about what I feel for you. It is odd how completely our feelings change. No one can tell the effort it was to me to tell you I loved you – why I do not know, but it made me gasp for breath, and now it is absolutely pleasure to me to tell it to you and bore you with it in every form, and I should like to write it in big letters I LOVE YOU all across the page by way of emphasis. I know you will think me very childish and be shaken in your early notion that I am intellectual, but I cannot help it. This is my state of mind.

To change the subject, what is the particular advantage of being rubbed at *Edinburgh*? Since yesterday I have made careful enquiries and am assured that the English can rub. Why not be rubbed in Somersetshire? Let the doctor mark the place and have a patch put to show where and let an able-bodied party in the West of England rub on the *same* place and surely it will be as well? Does the man's touch do good to disease like the King's?

By incredible researches in an old box I have found the poem I mentioned to you. I wish I had not, for I thought it was better. I have not seen it for several years and it is not so good as I fancied – perhaps not good at all – but I think you may care to read it and you can't read it unless I send it and therefore I do send it. The young lady's name is Orithyia. The Greek legend is that she was carried away by the north wind. I have chosen to believe that she was in love with the north wind, but I am not aware that she ever declared her feelings explicitly in any document. By the way, you have. I have just read your letter in that light and I go about murmuring, 'I have made that dignified girl *commit* herself, I have, I have', and then I vault over the sofa with exultation. Those are the feelings of the person you have connected yourself with. *Please* don't be offended at my rubbish. Sauciness is my particular line. I am always rude to everybody I respect. I could write to you of the deep and serious feelings which I hope you believe really are in my heart, but my pen jests of itself and always will.

Yours with the fondest and deepest love,
Walter Bagehot

SEPARATIONS

LADY PELHAM to SIR JOHN PELHAM

[1399]

My dear Lord,

I recommend me to your high lordship, with heart and body and all my poor might. And with all this I thank you as my dear Lord, dearest and best beloved of all earthly lords. I say for me, and thank you, my dear Lord, with all this that I said before for your comfortable letter that you sent me from Pontefract, that came to me on Mary Magdalen's day; for by my troth I was never so glad as when I heard by your letter ye were strong enough with the Grace of God to keep you from the malice of your enemies. And, dear Lord, if it like to your high Lordship that as soon as ye might that I might hear of your gracious speed, which God Almighty continue and increase. And, my dear Lord, if it like you to know *my* fare, I am here laid by in a manner of a siege with the County of Sussex, Surrey and a great parcel of Kent, so that I may not go out nor no victuals get me, but with much hazard. Wherefore, my dear, if it like you by the advice of your wise counsel for to set remedy to the salvation of your castle and withstand the malice of the shires aforesaid. And also that ye be fully informed of the great malice-workers in these shires which have so despitefully wrought to you, and to your castle, to your men, and to your tenants; for this country have they wasted for a great while.

Farewell, my dear Lord! the Holy Trinity keep you from your enemies, and soon send me good tidings of you. Written at Pevensey, in the castle, on St. Jacob's day last past, by your own poor J. Pelham. To my true Lord.

ALEXANDER HAMILTON to MRS HAMILTON

August, 1781.

In my last letter I informed you that there was a greater prospect of activity now, than there had been heretofore. I did this to prepare your mind for an event, which, I am sure, will give you pain. I begged your father at the same time to intimate to you by degrees the probability of its taking place. I used this method to prevent a surprise which might be too severe to you. A part of the army, my dear girl, is going to Virginia, and I must of necessity be separated at a much greater distance from my beloved wife. I cannot announce the fatal necessity without feeling everything that a fond husband can feel. I am unhappy; – I am unhappy beyond expression. I am unhappy because I am to be so remote from you; because I am to hear from you less frequently than I am accustomed to do. I am miserable because I know you will be so; I am wretched at the idea of flying so far from you, without a single hour's interview, to tell you all my pains and all my love. But I cannot ask permission to visit you. It might be thought improper to leave my corps at such a time and upon such an occasion. I must go without seeing you, – I must go without embracing you : – alas! I must go. But let no idea, other than of the distance we shall be asunder, disquiet you. Though I said the prospects of activity will be greater, I said it to give your expectations a different turn, and prepare you for something disagreeable. It is ten to one that our views will be disappointed, by Cornwallis retiring to South Carolina by land. At all events, our operations will be over by the latter end of October, and I will fly to my home. Don't mention I am going to Virginia.

King Henry VIII to Anne Boleyn

[1528]

My mistress and friend,

I and my heart put ourselves in your hands, begging you to recommend us to your good grace and not to let absence lessen your affection, for it were great pity to increase their pain, seeing that absence does that sufficiently and more than I could ever have thought possible; reminding us of a point in astronomy, which is that the longer the days are the farther off is the sun and yet the hotter; so is it with our love, for although by absence we are parted it nevertheless keeps its fervency, at least in my case and hoping the like of yours; assuring you that for myself the pang of absence is already too great, and when I think of the increase of what I must needs suffer it would be well nigh intolerable but for my firm hope of your unchangeable affection; and sometimes to put you in mind of this, and seeing that in person I cannot be with you, I send you now something most nearly pertaining thereto that is at present possible to send, that is to say, my picture set in a bracelet with the whole device which you already know; wishing myself in their place when it shall please you. This by the hand of

Your loyal servant and friend,

H Rex

Charles Stewart Parnell to Katharine O'Shea

Kilmainham,
October 14, 1881.

My Own Dearest Wifie,

I have found a means of communicating with you, and of your communicating in return.

Please put your letters into enclosed envelope, first putting them into an inner envelope, on the joining of which you can write your initials with a similar pencil to mine, and they will reach me all right. I am very comfortable here, and have a beautiful room facing the sun – the best in the prison. There are three or four of the best of the men in adjoining rooms with whom I can associate all day long, so that time does not hang heavy nor do I feel lonely. My only fear is about my darling Queenie. I have been racked with torture all today, last night, and yesterday, lest the shock may have hurt you or our child. Oh, darling, write or wire me as soon as you get this that you are well and will try not to be unhappy until you see your husband again. You may wire me here.

I have your beautiful face with me here; it is such a comfort. I kiss it every morning.

Your King.

BERT FIELDER to NELL FIELDER

[21 July 1915]

My Dearest Nell,

I think I may be able to keep here a few weeks yet, anyhow I've got hopes of staying until the Dardanelles job is over. . . . You ask me when the war is going to be over. Well, I will just tell you, only keep it secret. *In October.* You say we don't seem to be getting on very well out here; My Word if you only knew what a job we've got before us, just try to imagine a hill called Achi Baba, just fancy yourself at the bottom of a big hill with trenches and trenches piled on top of one another, made of concrete with thousands of Turks and machine-guns, five of these trenches we took one morning one after the other, but before we got to the first trench we left a good many of our chums behind, but it's no good stopping and the faster you can run the better chance you have of getting through the rain of bullets, and our boys went mad.

I have thought just lately what a lot of savages war turns us into, we see the most horrible sights of bloodshed and simply laugh at it. It seems to be nothing but blood, blood everywhere you go and on everything you touch, and you are walking amongst dead bodies all day and all night, human life seems to be of no value at all—you are joking with a chap one minute and the next minute you go to the back of the trench to do a job for yourself and then you see a little mound of earth with a little rough wooden cross on it with the name of the man you had been joking with a short time before. My dear Scrumps, I don't know whether I'm right in telling you this, because you worry so but I would not mention it only for the reason that I don't think I shall have any more of it, but I certainly *do* thank the One Above and you for your prayers at night together with our Boy for keeping me safe throughout it all.

Always you are both in my thoughts, I think of you both in that little kitchen by yourselves and know that you are thinking of me and wondering perhaps if you will ever see me come back again, every night at nine o'clock out here which is seven o'clock in England, I think that it is the Boy's bedtime and I always can picture him kneeling in his cot saying his prayers after Mummy. But 'Cheer up', my Scrumps, this will all end soon and we shall be together again and carry on the old life once more.

My dear Scrumps, I wonder if the Boy still thinks of the gun I promised to bring him home, I got hold of two Turks' guns to bring home and after keeping them for about two weeks, I got wounded and then of course I lost them as I did everything else. I might also say that the Deal Battalion have all lost their bags again, they were coming from the ship in a barge and a Turk shell hit the barge, so they sank to the bottom of the Dardanelles. The Naval Division is pretty well cut up, especially the Marines, they can only make 3 btns out of 4 even after the last lot came out from England. I think there is some move on to withdraw the Marines and Naval Division from the Dardanelles also the other troops which were in the first part of the fighting as they are in a bad state and I expect we'll get a quiet job as garrison for some place. I expect by this time you have got General Hamilton's report of the fighting here, my dear Scrumps I think I will wind up now as I've just looked at the watch and its a quarter to eleven. I've been writing ever since nine o'clock, so Night Night and God Bless you.

TAUS to APOLLONIUS

[c. Second century, Roman]

Taus to Apollonius her Lord, very many greetings. Before all else I salute you, Master, and always pray for your health. I was not a little distressed, Lord, to hear you'd been ill, but thanks be to all the gods because they keep you safe and sound. I beg you, Lord, if it seems good to you, to send for me, else I die because I don't behold you daily. Would that I could fly and come to you and make obeisance to you. For I'm torn by anxiety when I don't see you. So be kind and send for me. Goodbye Lord. All is well with us.

Epeiph 24.

ANTON CHEKHOV to OLGA KNIPPER

Yalta, January 20, 1903

What have you decided? What will you tell me about Switzerland? It seems to me that we could take a very good trip. On the way we could stop off at Vienna, Berlin, etc., go to the theaters. Eh? What do you think?

Savina is putting on my old skit, 'The Jubilee', at her benefit. Again they will say that this is a new play and they will gloat.

Today it's sunny, a bright day, but I sit indoors because

Altschuller has forbidden me to go out. My temperature, by the way, is completely normal.

You keep writing, my own, that your conscience is tormenting you because you are living in Moscow and not with me in Yalta. Well, what can we do about it, my dear one? Judge the matter properly: if you were to stay with me in Yalta all through the winter your life would be marred and I would feel the pangs of remorse, which would hardly improve matters for us. I knew, of course, that I was marrying an actress – that is, when I married I realized clearly that you would be spending your winters in Moscow. I do not consider myself passed over or wronged one millionth of a degree – on the contrary, it seems to me that everything is going well, or the way it ought to go and so, darling, don't disconcert me by your remorse. In March we shall start living happily once more and, once more, won't be feeling the loneliness we are feeling now. Calm down, my own, don't be agitated, live, and hope. Hope, and nothing more.

The supplement to *Plowed Land* has arrived: my short stories, with a portrait and, under the portrait, a wretchedly executed facsimile of my signature.

I am working now; probably I won't be writing you every day. Do forgive me.

Let's go abroad. Let's!

Your spouse,

A.

KING CHARLES I to THE QUEEN-CONSORT, HENRIETTA MARIA

Oxford, 9th of April [1645]

Dear Heart,

Though it be an uncomfortable thing to write by a slow messenger, yet all occasions of this which is now the only way of conversing with thee are so welcome to me as I shall be loth to lose any; but expect neither news nor public business from me by this way of conveyance. Yet, judging thee by myself, even these nothings will not be unwelcome to thee, though I should chide thee – which if I could I would – for thy too sudden taking alarms.

I pray thee consider, since I love thee above all earthly things, and that my contentment is inseparably conjoined with thine, must not all my actions tend to serve and please thee? If thou knew what a life I lead (I speak not in respect of the common distractions), even in point of conversation, which in my mind is the chief joy or vexation of one's life, I dare say thou wouldest pity me. For some are too wise, others too foolish, some too busy, others too reserved, many fantastic. . . .

I confess thy company hath perhaps made me, in this, hard to be pleased, but not less to be pitied by thee, who art the only cure for this disease. The end of all is this, to desire thee to comfort me as often as thou canst with thy letters. And dost not thou think that to know particulars of thy health, and how thou spendest thy time, are pleasing subjects unto me, though thou hast no other business to write of?

Believe me, sweet heart, thy kindness is as necessary to comfort my heart as thy assistance is for my affairs.

Thine

HONORÉ DE BALZAC to COUNTESS HANSKA

Dresden, October 21st, 1843.
I leave to-morrow, my seat is reserved, and I am going to finish my letter, because I have to put it in the post myself; my head is like an empty pumpkin, and I am in a state which disquiets me more than I can say. If I am thus in Paris, I shall have to return. I have no feeling for anything, I have no desire to live, I have no longer got the slightest energy, I seem to have no will-power left.

... I will write to you from Mayence, if I am better; but, for the moment, I can only paint my situation like Fontenelle, the centenarian, explained his, as a *difficulty of existing.* I have not smiled since I left you. This is translated in English by the word 'spleen'; but this is the spleen of the heart, and it is far more serious, for it is a double spleen.

Adieu, dear star, a thousand times blessed! There will perhaps come a moment when I shall be able to express to you the thoughts which oppress me. To-day I can only say that I love you too much for my repose, because after this August and September, I feel that I can only live near to you, and that your absence, is death— Ah! how happy I would be to walk and talk with you, in that little garden raised so daintily at the end of the bridge of Troisk, and where there are nothing yet but broomsticks, under the pretext that one day they will put trees in their place. For me, it is the most beautiful garden in Europe, meaning, of course, when you were there. There are instants I see again perfectly the least little objects which surround you; I look at the cushion bordered with a design in shape of black lace, upon which you rest, and I count the points of it. ... What a power and what happiness there is in these returns to a past which one thus sees anew; in those moments it is more than life, for it has held an entire life in that hour, torn from the real existence, to the benefit of the remembrances which inundate my soul in torrents. What sweetness and what force is there not in the simple thought of certain material objects, which have hardly attracted the attention in the happy days of the past; and how happy I feel myself at having this feeling. Adieu! I am going to take my letter to the post. A thousand tendernesses to your child a thousand times blessed; my friendly greetings to Lirette, and to you everything that is in my heart, my soul, and my brain. ...

(In going to put this one in the post.) If you knew what emotion seizes me when I throw one of these packets in the box.

My soul flies towards you with these papers; I say to them like a crazy man, a thousand things; like a crazy man I think that they go towards you to repeat them to you; it is impossible for me to understand how these papers impregnated by me will be, in eleven days, in your hands, and why I remain here. . . .

FAREWELLS

[1535]

Our Lord bless you, good daughter, and your good husband, and your little boy, and all yours, and all my children, and all my godchildren and all our friends. Recommend me when ye may to my good daughter Cicely, whom I beseech our Lord to comfort. And I send her my blessing, and to all her children, and pray her to pray for me. I send her a handkerchief: and God comfort my good son her husband. My good daughter Dauncey hath the picture in parchment that you delivered me from my Lady Coniers, her name is on the backside. Shew her that I heartily pray her that you may send it in my name to her again, for a token from me to pray for me. I like special well Dorothy Colly, I pray you be good unto her. I would wit whether this be she that you wrote me of. If not, yet I pray you be good to the other as you may in her affliction, and to my good daughter Joan Aleyn too. Give her, I pray you, some kind answer, for she sued hither to me this day to pray you be good to her. I cumber you, good Margaret, much, but I would be sorry if it should be any longer than tomorrow. For it is Saint Thomas' even and the Utas of Saint Peter; and therefore tomorrow long I to go to God: it were a day very meet and convenient for me. I never liked your manner toward me better than when you kissed me last: for I love when daughterly love and dear charity hath no leisure to look to worldly courtesy. Farewell, my dear child, and pray for me, and I shall for you and all your friends, that we may merrily meet in Heaven. I thank you for your great cost. I send now to my good daughter Clement her algorism stone, and I send her and my godson, and all hers, God's blessing and mine. I pray you at time convenient recommend me to my good son John More. I liked well his natural fashion. Our Lord bless him and his good wife my loving daughter, to whom I pray him be good as he hath great cause: and that if the land of mine come to his hand he break not my will concerning his sister Dauncey. And our Lord bless Thomas and Austen and all that they shall have.

Anonymous Suicide Note

[Twentieth century]
No wish to die. One of the best of sports, which they all knew. Not in the wrong, the boys will tell you. This b---- at Palmer's Green has sneaked my wife, one of the best in the world; my wife, the first love in the world.

CAMILLE DESMOULINS to LUCILE DESMOULINS

On the 2nd Germinal, the II Decade,
at 5 o'clock in the morning 1 April, 1794
Beneficent slumber has helped me to obliterate my sufferings. When one sleeps, one has not the feeling of being in prison, one is free. Heaven had mercy on me. Only a moment ago, I saw you in my dream, I embraced you one after another. . . . Our little one had lost an eye, and I saw it in a bandage. And in my distress at this, I woke up. I found myself in my dungeon. Day was dawning. I saw you no more, my Lolotte, and could not hear you, for you and your mother, you had spoken to me, and Horace, without feeling his pain, had said, 'Papa, papa.' Oh, these cruel ones, who deprive me of the joy to hear these words, to see you and to make you

happy. For that was my only ambition and my only conspiracy. . . .

I have discovered a crack in my cell. I put my ear to it and heard a sigh. I hazarded a few words and heard the voice of a sick man suffering. He asked me for my name, which I told him. 'My God!' he exclaimed as he sank back on his couch. 'I am Fabre d'Eglantine. But you are here? Has, then, the counter-revolution been successful?' We did not dare to talk with one another, in order that hatred might not deprive us of the poor consolation and so that one might not hear us and separate us from one another, to place us in still closer confinement. Beloved, you cannot imagine what it means to be in the dark, without knowing the reason, without being interrogated, without a single newspaper. It means at the same time living and being dead. Or alive and to feel oneself in a coffin. They say that innocence is at rest and full of courage. Oh, my precious Lucile, that would be true, if one were God.

At this moment the Commissaries of the Republic came to interrogate me, whether I had conspired against the Republic. How ridiculous! How can they so insult the purest Republicism! I see the fate which awaits me. Farewell, my precious Lucile, my Lolotte, say farewell to my father for me. You see in me an example of the barbarity and ingratitude of man. As you see, my fear was well founded, my premonition right every time. But my last moments shall not dishonour you. I was the husband of a woman of divine virtue, I was a good husband, a good son, I would also have been a good father. I follow my brothers who have died for the Republic. I am certain to take with me the esteem and pity of all friends of virtue, of freedom, and of truth. I die at thirty-four years of age, and yet it is a miracle that I have passed through so many pitfalls of the Revolution during five years, and that I am still alive.

I rest my head with confidence on the pillow of my all too numerous writings, but they all breathe the same love of humanity, the same wish, to make my fellow citizens free and happy, those whom the axe of Saint-Just will not fall upon. I see that power intoxicates almost all men and that they will say with

Dionysius of Syracuse, 'Tyranny is a beautiful gift.' However, console yourself, disconsolate widow, Hector's widow, for the inscription on the grave of your unhappy Camille is more glorious; it is that of Cato and Brutus, the murderers of tyrants.

My beloved Lucile, I was born to make verses and to defend the unfortunate. In this hall, where I fight now for my life, I defended four years ago for whole nights a mother of ten children, who could find no advocate. In front of the same bench of jurors, who now murder me, I once appeared, when my father had already lost a great lawsuit, suddenly like a miracle in the midst of the judges. Then at least weeping was no crime. My emotional speech knew how to move them, and I won the case, which my father had already lost. Such a conspirator am I! I never was any other. I was born in order to make you happy, in order to create for us both, with your mother and my father and some intimate friends, a Tahiti. I dreamed the dreams of the Abbé Saint-Pierre. I dreamed of a republic, the idol of all men; I could not believe that men are so unjust and so cruel. How could I imagine that a jovial allusion toward colleagues in my writings could obliterate so many services? I do not conceal from myself that I fall as victim of those pleasantries and of my friendship for the unfortunate Danton. I thank my murderers for this death with him. . . .

My colleagues, my friends, the whole 'mountain', which, with the exception of a few, have encouraged me, congratulated me, kissed me, pressed my hand in thanks, have been so cowardly as to desert me. Those who have said so much to me, and even those who condemned my newspaper, none of them can seriously consider me a conspirator. The freedom of the press and opinion has no longer any defenders, we will die as the last republicans, even though we had to pierce ourselves with our own swords like Cato, if there had been no guillotine.

Pardon me, my dear one, my true life, that I lost when we were separated, for occupying myself with memory. I had far better busy myself in making you forget. My Lucile, my dear Louploup, my darling, I implore you, do not call upon me; your cries will rend my heart even at the bottom of my grave. Care for your little one; live for my Horace; speak to him of me. Tell him hereafter what he cannot now understand, that I should have loved him well. Notwithstanding my punishment, I believe there is a God. My blood will wash out my faults, my human weakness, and for the good I have done, for my virtues, my love of Liberty, God will reward me. I shall see you again one day. O Lucile! . . . Feeling as I do, is death so great a misfortune, since it delivers me from the sight of so many enemies?

Good-bye, Louploup, my life, my soul, my heaven on earth! I leave you to good friends – all the sensible and virtuous men who remain. Good-bye – Lucile, my Lucile, my dear Lucile. . . . The shores of life recede from me. I see you still, Lucile, my beloved. My bound hands embrace you, and my head as it falls rests its dying eyes upon you.

CATHERINE OF ARAGON to KING HENRY VIII

[1535]

My Lord and Dear Husband,

I commend me unto you. The hour of my death draweth fast on, and my case being such, the tender love I owe you forceth me, with a few words, to put you in remembrance of the health and safeguard of your soul, which you ought to prefer before all worldly matters, and before the care and tendering of your own body, for the which you have cast me into many miseries and yourself into many cares.

For my part I do pardon you all, yea, I do wish and devoutly pray God that He will also pardon you.

For the rest I commend unto you Mary, our daughter, beseeching you to be a good father unto her, as I heretofore desired. I entreat you also, on behalf of my maids, to give them marriage-portions, which is not much, they being but three. For all my other servants, I solicit a year's pay more than their due, lest they should be unprovided for.

Lastly, do I vow, that mine eyes desire you above all things.

CHIDIOCK TICHBORNE to AGNES TICHBORNE

[1586]

To ye most lovinge wife alive, I commend me unto her and desire God to blesse her with all happiness, pray for her dead husband and be of good comfort, for I hope in Jesus Christ this morninge, to see the face of my Maker and redeemer in the most joyfull throan of his glorious kingdome, Commende me to all my friends and desire them to pray for me, and in all charitie to pardon me, if I have offended them, Commend me to my six Sisters poore desolate soules; advise them to serve god, for without him no goodness is to be expected here, were it possible, my little Sister Babb, the darlinge of my race might be bred by her, god would rewarde her; but I do her wronge I confesse that hath my desolate negligence too litle for her selfe, to add a further charge unto her. Deere wife forgive me, that hath by these meanes impoverished her fortunes; patience and pardon good wife I crave, make of these our necesseties a virtue, and lay no further burthen on my necke than hath alreadie borne, there be certaine debts that I owe; because I knowe not the order of the Lawe. Piteouse it hath taken from me all, forfeited by my course of offense to Her Majesty.

I cannot advise ye to benefite me herein, but if there fallout wherewithal lett them be discharged for godes sake. I will not that you should trouble yo.selfe with the performance of these matters, my owne heart, but make it knowne to my uncles and desire them, for the honour of god and ease of their sowls, to take care of them, as they may and specially care of my Sisters bringing opp. . . .

Now Sweet Cheeke, what is left now to bestowe on thee, a Small joynture, a Small recompense for thy deserving, these legacies followinge to be thine owne. God of his infinite goodnes give thee grace alwaies to remaine his true and faithfull Servant who, that through the merites of his bitter and blessed passion, thou maiest become . . . of his kingdom with the blessed women in heaven. . . . May the Holy Ghost comfort thee with all necessaries for the wealth of thy soul in the World to come, where untill it shall please almighty god I meete thee, farewell lovinge Wife, ffarewell the dearest to me on all ye Earthe, ffarewell, by the hand from the hearte of the most faithfull lovinge husbande

Chideock Ticheburn

SIR WALTER RALEGH to ELIZABETH RALEGH

[1603]

You shall now receive (my deare wife) my last words in these my last lines. My love I send you that you may keep it when I am dead, and my councell that you may remember it when I am no more. I would not by my will present you with sorrowes (dear Besse) let them go to the grave with me and be buried in the dust. And seeing that it is not Gods will that I should see you any more in this life, beare it patiently, and with a heart like thy selfe.

First, I send you all the thankes which my heart can conceive, or my words can reherse for your many travailes, and care taken for me, which though they have not taken effect as you wished, yet my debt to you is not the lesse: but pay it I never shall in this world.

Secondly, I beseech you for the love you beare me living, do not hide your selfe many dayes, but by your travailes seeke to helpe your miserable fortunes and the right of your poor childe. Thy mourning cannot availe me, I am but dust.

Thirdly, you shall understand, that my land was conveyed *bona fide* to my childe; the writings were drawne at midsummer was twelve months, my honest cosen Brett can testify so much, and Dolberry too, can remember somewhat therein. And I trust my blood will quench their malice that have cruelly murthered me: and that they will not seek also to kill thee and thine with extreame poverty.

To what friend to direct thee I know not, for all mine have left me in the true time of tryall. And I perceive that my death was determined from the first day. Most sorry I am God knowes that being thus surprised with death I can leave you in no better estate. God is my witnesse I meant you all my office of wines or all that I could have purchased by selling it, halfe of my stuffe, and all my jewels, but some one for the boy, but God hath prevented all my resolutions. That great God that ruleth all in all, but if you live free from want, care for no more, for the rest is but vanity. Love God, and begin betimes to repose your selfe upon him, and therein shall you finde true and lasting riches, and endlesse comfort: for the rest when you have travailed and wearied your thoughts over all sorts of worldly cogitations, you shall but sit downe by sorrowe in the end.

Teach your son also to love and feare God while he is yet young, that the feare of God may grow with him, and then God will be a husband to you, and a father to him; a husband and a father which cannot be taken from you.

Baily oweth me 200 pounds, and Adrian Gilbert 600. In Jersey I also have much owing me besides. The arrearages of the wines will pay my debts. And howsoever you do, for my soules sake, pay all poore men. When I am gone, no doubt you shall be sought for by many, for the world thinkes that I was very rich. But take heed of the pretences of men, and their affections, for they last not but in honest and worthy men, and no greater misery can befall you in this life, than to become a prey, and afterwards to be despised. I speake not this (God knowes) to dissuade you from marriage, for it will be best for you, both in respect of the world and of God. As for me, I am no more yours, nor you mine, death hath cut us asunder: and God hath divided me from the world, and you from me.

Remember your poor childe for his father's sake, who chose you, and loved you in his happiest times. Get those letters (if it be possible) which I writ to the Lords, wherein I sued for my life: God is my witnesse it was for you and yours that I desired life, but it is true that I disdained my self for begging of it: for know it (my deare wife) that your son is the son of a true man, and one who in his owne respect despiseth death and all his misshapen & ugly formes.

I cannot write much, God he knows how hardly I steale this time while others sleep, and it is also time that I should separate my thoughts from the world. Begg my dead body which living was denied thee; and either lay it at Sherburne (and if the land continue) or in Exeter-Church, by my Father and Mother; I can say no more, time and death call me away.

The everlasting God, powerfull, infinite, and omnipotent God, That Almighty God, who is goodnesse it selfe, the true life and true light keep thee and thine: have mercy on me, and teach me to forgive my persecutors and false accusers, and send us to meet in his glorious Kingdome. My deare wife farewell. Blesse my poore boy. Pray for me, and let my good God hold you both in his armes.

Written with the dying hand of sometimes thy Husband, but now alasse overthrowne.

Yours that was, but now not my own.

Walter Rawleigh

UNIONS

JANE WELSH CARLYLE to THOMAS CARLYLE

Craigenvilla, Edinburgh: Monday, 24 August, 1857

Oh, my dear! What a magnificent book this is going to be! The best of all your books. I say so, who never flatter, as you are too well aware; and who am 'the only person I know that is always in the right!' So far as it is here before me, I find it forcible and vivid, and sparkling as 'The French Revolution,' with the geniality and composure and finish of 'Cromwell' – a wonderful combination of merits! And how you have contrived to fit together all those different sorts of pictures, belonging to different sorts of times, as compactly and smoothly as a bit of the finest mosaic! Really one may say, of these two first books at least, what Helen said of the letters of her sister who died – you remember? – 'So splendidly put together one would have thought that hand couldn't have written them!'

It was the sheets that hindered me from writing yesterday; though I doubt if a letter posted at Morningside (the Scotch *Campo Santo*) yesterday (Sunday) would have reached you sooner than if posted to-day. Certainly it is a devil of a place for keeping the Sunday, this! Such preaching and fasting, and 'touting and praying,' as I was never before concerned in! But one never knows whence deliverance is to come any more than misfortune. I was cut out of all, or nearly all, my difficulties yesterday by the simple providential means of – a bowel complaint! It was reason enough for staying away from church; excuse enough for declining to be read to; and the loss of my dinner was entirely made up for by the loss of my appetite! Nothing could have happened more opportunely! Left at home with Pen (the cat), when they had gone every one to her different 'Place of Worship,' I opened my desk to write you a letter. But I would just take a look at the sheets first. Miss Jess had put a second cover on the parcel, and forwarded it by railway on Saturday night; and I had not been able to read then, by the gas-light, which dazzles my eyes. It is one of the little peculiarities of this house that there isn't a candle allowed in it of any sort – wax, dip, moulded, or composite! Well, I took up the sheets and read 'here a little and there a little,' and then I began at the beginning and never could stop till I had read to the end, and pretty well learnt it by heart. I was still reading when Church came out, and so my letter got nipt in the bud. If it is so interesting for me, who have read and heard so many of the stories in it before, what must it be to others to whom it is all new? the matter as well as the manner of the narrative! Yes, you shall see, it will be the best of all your books – and small thanks to it! It has taken a doing! . . .

Yours affectionately,
Jane W. Carlyle

THOMAS CARLYLE to JANE WELSH CARLYLE

Chelsea,
13 July, 1846

Dearest,

I hope the Seaforth Post-Office will exert itself, and endeavour to be punctual on this occasion for once! I send thee a poor little Card-case, a small memorial of Bastille-day, and of another day also very important to me and thee! My poor little Jeannie, no heart ever wished another more truly 'many happy returns'; or if 'happy returns' are not in our vocabulary then 'wise returns', wise and true and brave, which after all are the only 'happiness', as I conjecture, that we have any right to look for in this segment of Eternity that we are traversing together, thou and I. God bless thee, Darling; and know thou always, in spite of the chimeras and delusions that thou art dearer to me than any earthly creature. That *is* a fact, if it can be of any use to thy poor soul to know. And so accept my little Gift, and kiss it as I have done; and say, In the name of Heaven it shall yet all be well; and my poor Husband *is* the man I have always known him from of old, is and will be!

I meant to write a longer Letter; but the moments are counted for me; and I am nearly roasted to death before starting. Such a passage in that Steamer: it seems to me I will never set foot in one again. I *walked* out to Addiscombe on Saturday afternoon; carrying a clean shirt and comb in my pocket; and did very well with that luggage, and indeed very well altogether; the Lady 'sick'; Baring engaged in agricultural donothingisms; nobody else there at all: a very quiet time, and even considerable sleep and rest; but this horrid baking for two hours on the River has spoiled all! . . .

Adieu Dearest

T.

OLIVER CROMWELL to ELIZABETH CROMWELL

Dunbar, 4 September, 1650

For my beloved Wife Elizabeth Cromwell, at the Cockpit: These

My Dearest,

I have not leisure to write much, but I could chide thee that in many of thy letters thou writest to me, that I should not be unmindful of thee and thy little ones. Truly, if I love thee not too well, I think I err not on the other hand much. Thou art dearer to me than any creature; let that suffice.

The Lord hath showed us an exceeding mercy: who can tell how great it is. My weak faith hath been upheld. I have been in my inward man marvellously supported; though I assure thee, I grow an old man, and feel infirmities of age marvellously stealing upon me. Would my corruptions did as fast decrease. Pray on my behalf in the latter respect. The particulars of our late success Harry Vane or Gil: Pickering will impart to thee. My love to all dear friends. I rest thine,

Oliver Cromwell

OLIVER CROMWELL to ELIZABETH CROMWELL

Edinburgh, 3 May, 1651

For Elizabeth Cromwell, at the Cockpit.

My Dearest,

I could not satisfy myself to omit this post, although I have not much to write; yet indeed I love to write to my dear, who is very much in my heart. It joys me to hear they soul prospereth; the Lord increase His favours to thee more and more. The great good thy soul can wish is, That the Lord lift upon thee the light of His countenance, which is better than life. The Lord bless all thy good counsel and example to all those about thee, and hear all thy prayers, and accept thee always.

I am glad to hear thy son and daughter are with thee. I hope thou wilt have some good opportunity of good advice to him. Present my duty to my Mother, my love to all the family. Still pray for

Thine,
O. Cromwell

CZARINA ALEXANDRA to CZAR NICHOLAS II

My Very Precious One,

Good-bye, sweet Lovy!

Its great pain to let you go – worse than ever after the hard times we have been living & fighting through. But God who is all love & mercy has let the things take a change for the better, – just a little more patience & deepest faith in the prayers & help of our Friend – then all will go well. I am fully convinced that great & beautiful times are coming fór yr. reign & Russia. Only keep up your spirits, let no talks or letters pull you down – let them pass by as something unclean & quickly to be forgotten.

Show to all, that you are the Master & your will shall be obeyed – the time of great indulgence & gentleness is over – now comes your reign of will & power, & they shall be made to bow down before you & listen your orders & to work how & with whom you wish – obedience they must be taught, they do not know the meaning of that word, you have spoilt them by yr. kindness & all forgivingness.

Why do people hate me? Because they know I have a strong will & when am convinced of a thing being right (when besides blessed by *Gregory*), do not change my mind & that they can't bear. But its the bad ones.

Remember Mr. Philipps words when he gave me the image with the bell. As you were so kind, trusting & gentle, I was to be yr. bell, those that came with wrong intentions wld. not be able to approach me & I wld. warn you. Those who are afraid of me, don't look me in the eyes or are up to some wrong, never like me. – Look at the black ones – then Orlov & Drenteln – Witte – *Kokovtzev* – *Trepov*, I feel it too – *Makarov – Kaufmann – Sofia Ivanovna – Mary – Sandra* Obolensky, etc., but those who are good & devoted to you honestly & purely – love me, – look at the simple people & military. The good & bad clergy its all so clear & therefore no more hurts me as when I was younger. Only when one allows oneself to write you or me nasty impertinent letters – you must punish.

Ania told me about *Balaschov* (the man I always disliked). I understood why you came so awfully late to bed & why I had such pain & anxiety waiting. Please, Lovy, tell Frederiks to write him a strong *reprimand* (he & *Nicolai Mikhailovitch* & Vass make one in the club)– he has such a high court-rank & dares to write, unasked. And its not the first time – in bygone days I remember he did so too. Tear up the letter, but have him firmly reprimanded – tell *Voyeikov* to remind the old man – such a smack to a conceited member of the Council of the Empire will be very useful.

We cannot now be trampled upon. Firmness above all! – Now you have made *Trepov's* son A.D.C. you can insist yet more on his working with *Protopopov*, he must prove his gratitude. – Remember to forbid *Gurko* speaking & mixing himself into politics – it ruined *Nikolasha* & Alexeiev, – the latter God sent this illness clearly to save you fr. a man who was lossing his way & doing harm by listening to bad letters & people, instead of listening to yr. orders about the war & being obstinate. And one has set him against me – proof – what he said to old Ivanov. –

But soon all this things will blow over, its getting clearer & the weather too, which is a good sign, remember.

And our dear Friend is praying so hard for you – a man of God's near one gives the strength, faith & hope one needs so sorely. And others cannot understand this great calm of yours & therefore think you don't understand & try to ennervate, frighten & prick at you. But they will soon tire of it.

Should Mother dear write, remember the Michels are behind her. – Don't heed & take to heart – thank God, she is not here, but kind people find means of writing & doing harm. All is turning to the good – our Friends dreams means so much. Sweety, go to the *Moghilev* Virgin & find peace & strength there – look in after tea, before you receive, take Baby with you, quietly – its so calm there – & you can place yr. candels. Let the people see you are a christian Sovereign & don't be shy – even such an example will help others. –

How will the lonely nights be? I cannot imagine it. The consolation to hold you tightly clasped in my arms – it lulled the pain of soul & heart & I tried to put all my endless love, prayers & faith & strength into my caresses. So inexpressibly dear you are to me, husband of my heart. God bless you & my Baby treasure – I cover you with kisses; when sad, go to Baby's room & sit a bit quietly there with his nice people. Kiss the beloved child & you will feel warmed & calm. All my love I pour out to you, Sun of my life. –

Sleep well, heart & soul with you, my prayers around you – God & the holy Virgin will never forsake you—

Ever your very, very,

Own

ANTON CHEKHOV to OLGA KNIPPER

Yalta,

September 1, 1902

My dear one, my own,

Once again I have had an odd letter from you. Once again you blame my poor head for anything and everything. Who told you that I don't want to return to Moscow, that I've left for good and won't be going back this fall? Didn't I write you in plain and simple language that I would definitely be coming in September and would live with you until December? Well, didn't I? You accuse me of not being frank, yet you forget everything I write or say to you. I am at a loss as to what I should do with my wife or how I should write her. You write that you tremble when you read my letters, that it's time for us to part, that there's something you fail to understand in all this. . . . It seems to me, darling, the guilty party in all this mess is neither you nor I, but someone else, someone you've had a talk with. Someone has instilled in you a mistrust of my words and feelings; everything seems suspicious to you – and there's nothing I can do about it, nothing at all. I won't try to dissuade you or convince you I'm right, for that's useless. You write that I am capable of living with you in complete silence, that I need only the amiable woman in you and that as a human being you are alien to me and isolated. Dearest darling, you are my wife, when are you finally going to understand that? You are the person who is closest and dearest to me; I loved you infinitely, I still love you, and you describe yourself as an 'amiable' woman who is alien and isolated. . . . Well then, have it your way, if you must.

My health is better, but I've been coughing violently. There hasn't been any rain, and it's hot. Masha is leaving on the fourth and will be in Moscow on the sixth. You write that I will show Masha your letter. Thanks for the confidence. By the way, Masha is in no way to blame. You'll see that for yourself sooner or later.

I've begun reading Naidenov's play. I don't like it. I have no desire to read it through to the end. Send me a wire when you move to Moscow. I'm tired of writing to other people's addresses. Don't forget my fishing rod; wrap it up in paper. Be cheerful and don't mope, or at least try to look cheerful. Sofya Sredina came to see me; she had a lot of things to say, none of which were interesting. She knew all about your illness and about who stayed by your side and who didn't. The elder Madame Sredina is already in Moscow.

If you plan on drinking wine, let me know and I'll bring you some. Write and tell me if you have any money or if you can make do until my arrival. Chaleyeva is living in Alupka; she's doing very poorly.

We've been catching mice.

Write and tell me what you're doing, which roles you're playing again and which new ones you're rehearsing. You're not as lazy as your husband, are you?

Darling, be my wife, be my friend, write good letters, stop spreading melancholera, don't torture me. Be a kind, gentle wife, the kind you really are anyway. I love you more strongly than ever before, and as a husband I am blameless. Why can't you finally understand that, my joy, my little scribble?

[140]

Good-bye. Keep well and cheerful. Be sure to write me every day. I kiss you, kewpie, I hug you.

Yours,

A.

BENJAMIN RUSH to JULIA RUSH

Philadelphia, 29 May, 1776

My Dearest Life,

I have wept over both your letters. I thank you for your tender regard for my welfare in the first, and I rejoice to discover such a flow of spirits in the second of them. Our cause prospers in every county of the province. The hand of heaven is with us. Did I not think so, I would not have embarked in it. You have everything to hope and nothing to fear from the part which duty to God, to my country, and to my conscience have led me to take in our affairs. The measures which I have proposed have hitherto been so successful that I am *constrained* to believe I act under the direction of providence. God knows I seek his honour and the best interests of my fellow creatures supremely in all I am doing for my country. General Mifflin and all the delegates from the independent colonies rely chiefly upon (*me*) Colonel McKean and a few more of us for the salvation of this province. It would be treason in any one of us to desert the cause at the present juncture. I often anticipate the joy with which we shall welcome the establishment of liberty and the return of peace to our country – when freedom shall prevail without licentiousness, government without tyranny, and religion without superstition, bigotry, or enthusiasm. Oh happy days! To have contributed even a mite to hasten or complete them is to rise above all the Caesars and Alexanders of the world.

Tuesday morning. Had a levee of clergymen to breakfast with

[141]

me. Had a visit from Mrs. Stamper, who took Adam home with her after leaving much love for you. Had the pleasure of an old schoolmate's company to drink tea with me. We spent two years in Edinburgh together. His name is Brown. WEDNESDAY. Entertained Mr. Rittenhouse, Colonel Trumbull, and Major Mifflin (cousin to the General) with a plain family dinner. Expected General Gates and General Mifflin, who disappointed me. Spent the evening in company with five of the back county assemblymen – *all* firm independents. Heard from my brother that 7,000 men has risen in arms in Maryland to compel their convention to declare independence. *All's for the best.* Adieu, my sweet Julia. My heart glows with an affection for you at this instant so tender, so delicate, and so refined that I want words to express it. Once more adieu. I have only to command you in my prayers to the protection and mercies of heaven before I close the day. I anticipate with you the pleasure we shall enjoy when we have no third person to break in upon our sweet house of social and conjugal happiness. I have a thousand things to say to you. I think, write, talk, work, love – all, all – only for you. Adieu. Love to all the family. Yours,

BR

JILL FURSE to LAURENCE WHISTLER

[November, 1944]

I should never have been able to say that about gaiety, except from living with you. When I was small I was gay, but it has taken me nearly all the years in between to recover it, because no one allowed me to believe it until you gave it back to me. But it is true and so important.

There's such a lot to say – but I suppose we shall have enough time in our lives – other beds and other firesides. I need all eternity to love you in. It's when I think of that – often here alone by the bedside candle – that I find all this separation hard to bear, though with my reason I *know* it's not time that matters.

Yesterday I actually struggled up to Newcombe in one of those blue abstracted afternoons of late autumn when the sky seems intensely far away and absorbed in itself. . . . Beloved – the days go on. I do not miss you, for you have given me so much that I still feel I am with you. How inevitably one thing flowers out of another. I think we could not have had the harmony of this leave without the shared grief of the previous one. I still cannot quite get over God letting us be together just then. Something happened to our love then . . . I hope you won't think this probing too much. I love being *aware* of increase, and I can't bear to feel I might miss even one fraction of a detail.

JOHN HERVEY, FIRST EARL OF BRISTOL, to ELIZABETH
HERVEY

Newmarket,
3 May, 1697

My ever-new Delight

Knowing how kind a welcome all my scribbles meet with where they are addressed, neither heart nor hand can forbear, when any opportunity offers, to tell thee (tho' but by faint images of the former) how much I long to be in the place of this my harbinger, tho' perhaps thou mayst not see it but few hours before my arrival, which by the grace of God shall not be deferred one moment beyond Wednesday night; for all time is worse than lost that's spent where thou art not, thou only relish to all other pleasures. Tis you alone that sweetens life, and makes one wish the wings of time were clipt, which not only seems but really flies away too fast, much too fast, for those that love (shall I be vain and say) like us; for that instead of breeding a satiety in either, (you see I answer for you boldly,) the common fate of vulgar friendships, does but heighten the vehemence of our desires for a more intimate (if that be possible) and lasting enjoyment of each others conversation and love. Ah! my dear, how I could expatiate on this fruitful theme, were it not day-light already, which if thou knewest, I am sure, Pray, my dear, goe to bed, would be your request to, my dearest life, your faithful friend and constant lover, J. Hervey

---

ELIZABETH HERVEY to JOHN HERVEY, FIRST EARL OF BRISTOL

Bury,
25 October, 1697.

My dear dear love,

Ye hundred things I had to say when you left me, (& shoud endeed have so if you weir to be with me as many years,) must now be only to repeat how much and dearly I love you & have wanted you these few but tedious hours you have been absent. . . . Though I coud dwell for ever on this subject, yet I am sure you woud be angry with me if I did not tel ye wants those bills you left me to pay has put me in more then I thought for; but £20 will effectuially do my bisnes, which sum, if it is not easy for you to send, a note for Mr. Cook to receive it at London will do as well; for he can let me have that or any other sum I want; but I shall nead no more.

NATURE
OF LOVE

LUCREZIA BORGIA to PIETRO BEMBO

[1517]

My dearest Misser Pietro,

I know that the very expectation of something awaited is the greater part of satisfaction because the hope of possessing it lights up desire. The rarer it is, the more beautiful it seems, the commoner, the less so. I decided to put off writing to you until this moment, with the result that by awaiting some exquisite reward to your most exquisite letters, you have become the source of your own satisfaction; you are both creditor and payer.

Nevertheless I have in two of my letters, confessed to Monsignor Thesauriero* of my debt to you and this may have constituted no small part of that which I can pay. As far as the rest is concerned, I do not believe that I can be held bound. In your letters you express with such ease all that you feel for me, but, I, just because I feel so well disposed towards you, am unable to do so. It is this feeling of powerlessness which absolves me from the debt. However as it would be unsuitable for me to be both prosecutor and judge of my own cause, I submit to the weighty judgement of the aforesaid Monsignor Thesauriero, commending myself to his Lordship and you. Ferrara the seventh day of August.

Your own Duchess of Ferrara

*Thesauriero is a pun on a title meaning both thesaurus and Treasurer.

MARCEL PROUST to ANTOINE BIBESCO

[1904]

My dear Antoine,

I am writing to you out of an exaggerated sense of conscience–
and the fear of continuing to be dishonest in simply replacing
with a different feeling one whose expression can persist in the
other person's mind as the statement of a constant truth – (what
style). It is unpleasant for me to write this to you, and moreover it
is perhaps not even true, if you are to understand by 'true'
something definitive, whereas what we have here is in the process
of becoming truth etc. I wanted to tell you that your new attitude
towards me (which is, by the way, quite understandable) – a lack
of frankness, or rather an unwillingness to share confidences or ask
questions, in a word, an avoidance of intimacy – has touched on
something within me which did not exist before I knew you,
which you have moulded, and which had grown into the habit of
no longer living autonomously, stretching the horizons of its
existence until they reached the boundaries of another being and
so continuously dissipating in this imperceptible extension of
itself the potential of its life for unfolding admirable or unworthy
acts as they happened, along with the reflection of the dramas
which it had chanced upon, and the secrets which had been
entrusted to it. Now, having lost my second ego (that is, you) as a
result of this new attitude of yours, I have been unable to alter the
shape which you have given the first (my own). And just as a river
whose natural progress is dammed up with a high and
impenetrable barrier will run in another direction in obedience to
the physical law of its flow, thereby to run to waste or to make
fertile new ground, so I have had to pour out to another those
confidences which you no longer wished to receive, and have had
to receive from this confidant the secrets which have become
essential to me since you have accustomed me to them. Enough: it
makes me blush with shame that I have allowed these confessions
to slip out.

Yours,
Marcel

VICTOR HUGO to ADÈLE FOUCHER

[1821]

Tonight (20 October)

This is a most important letter, Adèle; for everything between us henceforth will depend on the impression which it makes upon you. I will try to marshal some coherent ideas, and it is certainly not sleep which I shall have to fight against tonight. I am going to speak to you seriously and intimately, and I only wish that it could be in person, for then I could have your reply (which I shall await with great impatience) on the spot, and judge for myself from your expression the effect which my words are having on you, an effect which will be crucial in deciding our common future.

There is one word, Adèle, which we appear until now to have been afraid of using – the word *love*; nevertheless what I feel for you really is genuine love; the problem is one of knowing whether what you feel for me is also love. This letter will remove this doubt upon whose resolution my entire life depends.

Listen. Within us there is a being not composed of physical matter, like an exile inside our bodies which it must outlive for all eternity. This being, essentially purer and of a superior nature, is our soul. It is the soul which gives birth to all passions, all raptures, which conceives the notion of God and heaven. I speak of these things in a high-flown manner, but this is necessary in order to be understood unambiguously; I hope that this style does not seem strange to you, but we are talking of matters which demand simple but elevated language. I will continue. The soul, so superior to the body to which it is bound, would remain on earth in intolerable solitude, if it were not allowed to some extent to choose from among all the souls of other men a partner to share with it misery in this life and bliss in eternity. When two souls, which have sought each other for however long in the throng, have finally found each other, when they have seen that they are matched, are in sympathy and compatible, in a word, that they are alike, there is then established for ever between them a union, fiery and pure as they themselves are, a union which begins on earth and continues for ever in heaven. This union is love, true love, such as in truth very few men can conceive of, that love which is a religion, which deifies the loved one, whose life comes from devotion and passion, and for which the greatest sacrifices are the sweetest delights. This is the love which you inspire in me, which you are bound to feel one day for another, if, to my everlasting misfortune, you do not already feel it for me. Your soul is made to love with the purity and passion of angels; but perhaps it can only love another angel, in which case I must tremble with apprehension.

The world, Adèle, does not comprehend such passions which are the prerogative only of certain beings who are granted happiness like yours or misery like mine. For the world, love is nothing more than a carnal appetite, a vague inclination which indulgence sates and absence destroys. That is why you have heard it said, by a strange misuse of words, that the passions are ephemeral. Alas! Adèle, are you aware that the word 'passion' means 'suffering'? And do you believe, in all honesty, that there is any suffering in these love affairs of common men, which are apparently so turbulent, but in fact so insipid? No, immortal love is eternal, because the being which experiences it is immortal. It is our souls which love and not our bodies.

At this point, however, bear in mind that nothing should be carried to extremes. I am not claiming that our bodies are of no importance in the greatest of bonds. The good Lord has understood that, without physical intimacy, there could never be any intimacy of the soul, because two beings which love one another must to some extent share their thoughts and their deeds. This is one of the reasons why he has created the attraction of one sex for the other, which is the only indication of the divinity of marriage. Thus, in youth, the union of the flesh works to strengthen the union of souls, which, remaining young and indivisible, strengthens in its turn the union of the flesh in old age and continues after death.

Have no fears, therefore, Adèle, about continuing a love which it is no longer in the power of God himself to terminate. I love you with this love based not on physical attractions but on moral qualities, with this love which leads either to heaven or hell, which fills one's entire life with joy or bitterness. I have laid my soul bare to you, I have used a language which I only use when speaking to those who can understand it. Examine yourself carefully; see if love means to you what it means to me, see if my soul is truly the sister of yours. Pay no attention to what foolish people may say, or what the petty minds around you may think; look deep into yourself, follow your own conscience. If the ideas in this letter are clear to you, if you really love me as I love you, then, my Adèle, I am yours for life, yours for all eternity. If you fail to understand my love, if I seem over-dramatic to you, then farewell! For my part, nothing can await me but death, and death will hold no terrors for me when I have no further hope on earth. Do not think though that I shall kill myself without bringing some benefit to others; that would be selfish and cowardly when there are plague victims to care for and holy wars to fight. I shall take steps to ensure that the giving up of my life will be no less beneficial to others than pleasant to me.

Perhaps these ideas will seem a little morbid to you, since you are used to seeing me always with a smile on my face, and know nothing of the usual track of my thoughts.

Adèle, I shudder to say this, but I do not think that you love me with the same love that I have pledged to you, and which alone can satisfy me. If you loved me, would you expect, whatever you did, to receive the same sort of trust which you grant me so casually and which seems to me to betoken indifference? You are offended by my most reasonable questions, and ask if I am afraid that your behaviour might be reprehensible. If you loved me as I love you, Adèle, you would know that you could do any one of a thousand things without being guilty of crime or even wrongdoing, while still arousing the jealousy of my frail affections. Love as I have described it is something with exclusive rights. I ask no indulgence for my part, not even permission to glance at any other living woman; I merely expect that no man should dare lay any claim to my beloved. I may want none but her, but her I do want totally. A glance, a smile, a kiss from you are my greatest joys; do you believe that I could stand by and watch another share them? Does this over-sensitivity alarm you? If you loved me, it would please you. What further proof do you need of my devotion?

The more love is pure and fiery, the more possessive it is, the more adept at finding reasons for anxiety. I have always experienced it in this way. I recall how, some years ago, I almost instinctively shuddered when your younger brother spent a night by chance in the same bed as you. As I have grown older, pondered and observed men's behaviour, this tendency of mine has only increased. It will bring you pain, Adèle, for it ought to bring about your happiness and I can see, on the contrary, that it burdens you.

Speak without fear, decide whether or not you want me as I am. The things at stake are my future, which is nothing, and yours, which is all-important. Consider that, if you love me, no obstacle will be strong enough to stand in my way; if you do not love me, to acknowledge the fact will be a sure way of ridding yourself of me rapidly. I shall bear you no ill-will; I know a way of disappearing where one is soon forgotten by those who feel indifferent. It is a disappearance from which none returns.

One final word: if this long letter appears sad and demoralised, do not be surprised; yours was so cold. You feel that 'our passion is excessive'! Adèle! ... I sought solace in rereading some old letters of yours, but the difference between the old and the new was so marked that instead of finding solace ... Farewell.

GOPAL PURI to KAILASH PURI

Military Hospital
Malir Cantt,
Karachi.
15 August, 1942

My dearest Vino,

It was heavenly to pass two nights with you. I still feel although a thousand miles away I am living with you. I have kept your chuni [stole] under my pillow so that I have your flavour all the time with me. I hope we will be able to meet soon again and I am writing separately to your parents to send you here to spend few days in Karachi. This is a beautiful city. Clifton beach is glorious. The sea breeze towards the evening makes the place ever so delightful. Moonlit nights are really loveable. Please consider visiting next month. You will be free for your Easter holidays.

You must be wondering why I was so sad the first day I met you. The recent death of my uncle and my own family responsibilities made me think if I will ever be able to provide for you the comfort and luxuries to which you are accustomed in your parents home. You must realise that you are going to marry a poor man with heavy family responsibilities. My mother is our first duty. She needs all our love and protection. We will have to discharge our duty towards her together. Won't you agree this is the test of our love. Love does not lie only in gazing towards each other, but it is looking into our future together with four eyes. I think this is the test of our love. I certainly wish my brothers and sister to get higher education. You also have got to complete yours. The only thing I can give you is education. And what is love? It is nothing but unselfishness giving. In this case there is an item of selfishness also – because education will give you capacity to help me in discharging my responsibilities. So I want to exercise the right of my love right now. Won't you darling write an essay on love? or any other topic which may be uppermost in your mind and send me. This will keep your mind occupied with at least some of me. And I will have your writings to inspire me to live here alone for as long as I have to be here. I love you darling more than my life. Write soon.

Ever yours,
Gopal

Dorothy Osborne to William Temple

[c. 1652–4]

Sir,

You have furnished me now with arguments to convince my brother, if he should ever enter upon the dispute again. In earnest, I believed all this before, to die both together, 'twould but increase our misery, and add to that which is more already than we can well tell how to bear. You are more cruel than she in hazarding a life that's dearer to me than that of the whole world's besides, and which makes all the happiness I have or ever shall be capable of. Therefore, by all our friendship I conjure you and, by the power you have given me, command you, to preserve yourself with the same care that you would have me live. 'Tis all the obedience I require of you, and will be the greatest testimony you can give me of your faith. When you have promised me this, 'tis not impossible but I may promise you shall see me shortly; though my brother Peyton (who says he will come down to fetch his daughter) hinders me from making the journey in compliment to her. Yet I shall perhaps find business enough to carry me up to town. 'Tis all the service I expect from two girls whose friends have given me leave to provide for, that some order I must take for the disposal of them may serve for my pretence to see you; but then I must find you pleased and in good humour, merry as you were wont to be when we first met, if you will not have me show that I am nothing akin to my cousin Osborne's lady.

But what an age 'tis since we first met, and how great a change it has wrought in both of us; if there had been as great a one in my face, it would be either very handsome or very ugly. For God sake, when we meet, let us design one day to remember old stories in, to ask one another by what degrees our friendship grew to this height 'tis at. In earnest, I am lost sometimes with thinking on't; and though I can never repent the share you have in my heart, I know not whether I gave it you willingly or not at first. No, to speak ingenuously, I think you got an interest there a good while before I thought you had any, and it grew so insensibly, and yet so fast, that all the traverses it has met with since has served rather to discover it to me than at all to hinder it. By this confession you will see I am past all disguise with you, and that you have reason to be satisfied with knowing as much of my heart as I do myself. Will the kindness of this letter excuse the shortness on't? Pray be it! For I have twenty more, I think, to write, and the hopes I had of receiving one from you last night kept me from writing this when I had more time; or if all this will not satisfy, make your own conditions, so you do not return it me by the shortness of yours. Your servant kisses your hands, and I am

Your faithful.

JOHN KEATS TO FANNY BRAWNE

8 July [1819]

My sweet Girl,

Your Letter gave me more delight, than any thing in the world but yourself could do; indeed I am almost astonished that any absent one should have that luxurious power over my senses which I feel. Even when I am not thinking of you I receive your influence and a tenderer nature steeling upon me. All my thoughts, my unhappiest days and nights have I find not at all cured me of my love of Beauty, but made it so intense that I am miserable that you are not with me: or rather breathe in that dull sort of patience that cannot be called Life. I never knew before, what such a love as you have made me feel, was; I did not believe in it; my Fancy was affraid of it, lest it should burn me up. But if you will fully love me, though there may be some fire, 'twill not be more than we can bear when moistened and bedewed with Pleasures. You mention 'horrid people' and ask me whether it depend upon them, whether I see you again. Do understand me, my love, in this. I have so much of you in my heart that I must turn Mentor when I see a chance of harm beffaling you. I would never see any thing but Pleasure in your eyes, love on your lips, and Happiness in your steps. I would wish to see you among those amusements suitable to your inclinations and spirits; so that our loves might be a delight in the midst of Pleasures agreeable enough, rather than a resource from vexations and cares. But I doubt much, in case of the worst, whether I shall be philosopher enough to follow my own Lessons: if I saw my resolution give you a pain I could not. Why may I not speak of your Beauty, since without that I could never have lov'd you. I cannot conceive any beginning of such love as I have for you but Beauty. There may be a sort of love for which, without the least sneer at it, I have the highest respect and can admire it in others: but it has not the richness, the bloom, the full form, the enchantment of love after my own heart. So let me speak of you[r] Beauty, though to my own endangering; if you could be so cruel to me as to try elsewhere its Power. You say you are affraid I shall think you do not love me – in saying this you make me ache the more to be near you. I am at the diligent use of my faculties here, I do not pass a day without sprawling some blank verse or tagging some rhymes; and here I must confess, that, (since I am on that subject,) I love you the more in that I believe you have liked me for my own sake and for nothing else. I have met with women whom I really think would like to be married to a Poem and to be given away by a Novel. I have seen your Comet, and only wish it was a sign that poor Rice would get well whose illness makes him rather a melancholy companion: and the more so as so to conquer his feelings and hide them from me, with a forc'd Pun. I kiss'd your writing over in the hope you had indulg'd me by leaving a trace of honey

– What was your dream? Tell it me and I will tell you the interpretation thereof.

Ever yours, my love!

John Keats

Do not accuse me of delay – we have not here an opportunity of sending letters every day. Write speedily.

FRANÇOIS MARIE AROUET (VOLTAIRE) to OLYMPE DUNOYER

The Hague, 1713.

I am a prisoner here in the name of the King; they can take my life, but not the love that I feel for you. Yes, my adorable mistress, to-night I shall see you, and if I had to put my head on the block to do it. For Heaven's sake, do not speak to me in such disastrous terms as you write; you must live and be cautious; beware of madame your mother as of your worst enemy. What do I say? Beware of everybody, trust no one; keep yourself in readiness, as soon as the moon is visible; I shall leave the hotel incognito, take a carriage or a chaise, we shall drive like the wind to Scheveningen; I shall take paper and ink with me; we shall write our letters. If you love me, reassure yourself, and call all your strength and presence of mind to your aid; do not let your mother notice anything, try to have your picture, and be assured that the menace of the greatest tortures will not prevent me to serve you. No, nothing has the power to part me from you; our love is based upon virtue, and will last as long as our lives. Adieu, there is nothing that I will not brave for your sake; you deserve much more than that. Adieu, my dear heart!

Arouet

RICHARD STEELE to MARY SCURLOCK

[1707]

Madam,

It is the hardest thing in the world to be in love and yet attend to business. As for me, all who speak to me find me out, and I must lock myself up or other people will do it for me.

A gentleman asked me this morning, 'What news from Lisbon?' and I answered, 'She is exquisitely handsome.' Another desired to know when I had been last at Hampton Court. I replied, 'It will be on Tuesday come se'nnight. Prythee, allow me at least to kiss your hand before that day, that my mind may be in some composure. O love! –

'A thousand torments dwell about me!
Yet who would live to live without thee?'

Methinks I could write a volume to you; but all the language on earth would fail in saying how much and with what disinterested passion I am ever yours,

Rich. Steele

FRÉDÉRIC CHOPIN (?) to DELPHINE POTOCKA

[c. 1835]

Fidelina, my one and only beloved:

I will bore you once again with my thoughts on the subject of inspiration and creativity, but as you will perceive these thoughts are directly connected with you.

I have long reflected on inspiration and creativity and slowly, slowly I think I have discovered the essential nature of these gifts.

To me inspiration and creativity come only when I have abstained from a woman for a longish period. When, with passion, I have emptied my fluid into a woman until I am pumped dry then inspiration shuns me and ideas won't crawl into my head. Consider how strange and wonderful it is that the same forces which go to fertilise a woman and create a human being should go to create a work of art! Yet a man wastes this life-giving precious fluid for a moment of ecstasy.

The same is true of scholars who devote themselves to scientific pursuits or men who make discoveries. The formula is apparently a simple one: whatever the field, the creator must abjure woman – then the forces in his body will accumulate in his brain in the form of inspiration and he may give birth to a pure work of art.

Just think of it – sexual temptation and desire can be transmitted into inspiration! Of course I am speaking only of those who have ability and talent. A fool, living without a woman, will merely be driven insane by frustration. He can't create anything worthy of God or man.

On the other hand unrequited love and unfulfilled passion, sharpened by the image of one's beloved and carrying unbearable frustration with it, can contribute to creativity. I have observed this in Norwid [a Polish poet].

What about Mozart? I don't know, but I think his wife became ordinary food for him, his love and passion cooled, and he was therefore able to compose a great deal. I haven't heard of any love-affairs in Mozart's life.

Sweetest Fidelina, how much of that precious fluid, how many forces have I wasted on you! I have not given you a child and God only knows how many excellent inspirations, how many musical ideas have gone to perdition!

Operam et oleum perdidi [I wasted the time and the trouble]!!! Who knows what ballades, polonaises, perhaps an entire concerto, have been forever engulfed in your little D flat major [their code for the female organ, possibly because D flat is the black key between two white keys C and D]. I cannot reckon what might have been, since I have not composed anything for ever so long, immersed as I was in you and in love. Works which could have come to life, drowned in your sweetest little D flat major, so that you are filled with music and pregnant with my compositions!

Time flies, life runs on, no one can recapture wasted moments. It is with reason that the saints call woman the gate to hell!

No, no I take back this last sentence. I eat my words. I won't erase what I have just written because if I do so you'll bother me until I tell you what the erased words were. And I don't have time to write another letter.

To me you are the gate of paradise. For you I will renounce fame, creativity, everything. Fidelina, Fidelina – I long for you intensely and frightfully.

I'm shivering as if ants were running up my spine to my head. When you finally arrive in your diligence I will glue myself to you, so that for a whole week you won't be able to tear me away from the little D flat major, and to hell with inspiration and ideas. Let my composition disappear in the dark forever.

Ah! I have thought up a new musical name for the little D flat major. Shall we call it 'tacit' [expressed in musical notation by —]? I'll explain it to you at once: isn't a pause a hole in the melody? So this name is a musical term quite appropriate for the little D flat major.

Hoffmann just came and scattered to the wind the possibility of writing a letter. The pupils will shortly arrive as well, I will therefore finish, so that my letter can leave by today's mail. I kiss your beloved little body all over.

> Your most faithful Frédéric
> Your entirely faithful Frédéric
> Your *most* gifted pupil, one who has
> skilfully mastered the art of making love

P.S. I wasted time doing nothing yesterday and the letter did not leave, so I am adding to it.

I have just finished a Prelude.

TOTAL LOVE

LADY SHIGENARI to LORD KIMURA SHIGENARI

[Sixteenth century]

I know that when two wayfarers 'take shelter under the same tree and slake their thirst in the same river' it has all been determined by their karma from a previous life. For the past few years you and I have shared the same pillow as a man and wife who had intended to live and grow old together, and I have become as attached to you as your own shadow. This is what I believed, and I think this is what you have also thought about us.

But now I have learnt about the final enterprise on which you have decided and, though I cannot be with you to share the grand moment, I rejoice in the knowledge of it. It is said that [on the eve of his final battle] the Chinese general Hsiang Yü, valiant warrior though he was, grieved deeply about leaving Lady Yü, and that [in our own country] Kiso Yoshinaka lamented his parting from Lady Matsudono. I have now abandoned all hope about our future together in this world, and [mindful of their example] I have resolved to take the ultimate step while you are still alive. I shall be waiting for you at the end of what they call the road to death.

I pray that you may never, never forget the great bounty, deep as the ocean, high as the mountains, that has been bestowed upon us for so many years by our lord, Prince Hideyori.

To Lord Shigenari, Governor of Nagato

From His Wife

HELOISE to ABELARD

[Twelfth century]

... You know, beloved, as the whole world knows, how much I have lost in you, how at one wretched stroke of fortune that supreme act of flagrant treachery robbed me of my very self in robbing me of you; and how my sorrow for my loss is nothing compared with what I feel for the manner in which I lost you. Surely the greater the cause for grief the greater the need for the help of consolation, and this no one can bring but you; you are the sole cause of my sorrow, and you alone can grant me the grace of consolation. You alone have the power to make me sad, to bring me happiness or comfort; you alone have so great a debt to repay me, particularly now when I have carried out all your orders so implicitly that when I was powerless to oppose you in anything, I found strength at your command to destroy myself. I did more, strange to say – my love rose to such heights of madness that it robbed itself of what it most desired beyond hope of recovery, when immediately at your bidding I changed my clothing along with my mind, in order to prove you the sole possessor of my body and my will alike. God knows I never sought anything in you except yourself; I wanted simply you, nothing of yours. I looked for no marriage-bond, no marriage portion, and it was not my own pleasures and wishes I sought to gratify, as you well know, but yours. The name of wife may seem more sacred or more binding, but sweeter for me will always be the word mistress, or, if you will permit me, that of concubine or whore. I believed that the more I humbled myself on your account, the more gratitude I should win from you, and also the less damage I should do to the brightness of your reputation.

You yourself on your own account did not altogether forget this in the letter of consolation I have spoken of which you wrote to a friend; there you thought fit to set out some of the reasons I gave in trying to dissuade you from binding us together in an ill-starred marriage. But you kept silent about most of my arguments for preferring love to wedlock and freedom to chains. God is my witness that if Augustus, Emperor of the whole world, thought fit to honour me with marriage and conferred all the earth on me to possess for ever, it would be dearer and more honourable to me to be called not his Empress but your whore.

For a man's worth does not rest on his wealth or power; these depend on fortune, but worth on his merits. And a woman should realize that if she marries a rich man more readily than a poor one, and desires her husband more for his possessions than for himself, she is offering herself for sale. Certainly any woman who comes to marry through desires of this kind deserves wages, not gratitude, for clearly her mind is on the man's property, not himself, and she would be ready to prostitute herself to a richer man, if she could. This is evident from the argument put forward in the dialogue of Aeschines Socraticus by the learned Aspasia to Xenophon and his wife. When she had expounded it in an effort to bring about a reconciliation between them, she ended with these words: 'Unless you come to believe that there is no better man nor worthier woman on earth you will always still be looking for what you judge the best thing of all – to be the husband of the best of wives and the wife of the best of husbands.'

These are saintly words which are more than philosophic; indeed, they deserve the name of wisdom, not philosophy. It is a holy error and a blessed delusion between man and wife, when perfect love can keep the ties of marriage unbroken not so much through bodily continence as chastity of spirit. But what error permitted other women, plain truth permitted me, and what they thought of their husbands, the world in general believed, or rather, knew to be true of yourself; so that my love for you was the more genuine for being further removed from error. What king or philosopher could match your fame? What district, town or village did not long to see you? When you appeared in public, who did not hurry to catch a glimpse of you, or crane his neck and strain his eyes to follow your departure? Every wife, every young girl desired you in absence and was on fire in your presence; queens and great ladies envied me my joys and my bed.

You had besides, I admit, two special gifts whereby to win at once the heart of any woman – your gifts for composing verse and song, in which we know other philosophers have rarely been successful. This was for you no more than a diversion, a recreation from the labours of your philosophic work, but you left many love-songs and verses which won wide popularity for the charm of their words and tunes and kept your name continually on everyone's lips. The beauty of the airs ensured that even the unlettered did not forget you; more than anything this made women sigh for love of you. And as most of these songs told of our love, they soon made me widely known and roused the envy of many women against me. For your manhood was adorned by every grace of mind and body, and among the women who envied me then, could there be one now who does not feel compelled by my misfortune to sympathize with my loss of such joys? Who is there who was once my enemy, whether man or woman, who is not moved now by the compassion which is my due? Wholly guilty though I am, I am also, as you know, wholly innocent. It is not the deed but the intention of the doer which makes the crime, and justice should weigh not what was done but the spirit in which it is done. What my intention towards you has always been, you alone who have known it can judge. I submit all to your scrutiny, yield to your testimony in all things.

Tell me one thing, if you can. Why, after our entry into religion, which was your decision alone, have I been so neglected and forgotten by you that I have neither a word from you when you are here to give me strength nor the consolation of a letter in absence? Tell me, I say, if you can – or I will tell you what I think and indeed the world suspects. It was desire, not affection which bound you to me, the flame of lust rather than love. So when the end came to what you desired, any show of feeling you used to make went with it. This is not merely my own opinion, beloved, it is everyone's. There is nothing personal or private about it; it is the general view which is widely held. I only wish that it *were* mine alone, and that the love you professed could find someone to defend it and so comfort me in my grief for a while. I wish I could think of some explanation which would excuse you and somehow cover up the way you hold me cheap.

I beg you then to listen to what I ask – you will see that it is a small favour which you can easily grant. While I am denied your presence, give me at least through your words – of which you have enough and to spare – some sweet semblance of yourself. It is no use my hoping for generosity in deeds if you are grudging in words. Up to now I had thought I deserved much of you, seeing that I carried out everything for your sake and continue up to the present moment in complete obedience to you. It was not any sense of vocation which brought me as a young girl to accept the austerities of the cloister, but your bidding alone, and if I deserve no gratitude from you, you may judge for yourself how my labours are in vain. I can expect no reward for this from God, for it is certain that I have done nothing as yet for love of him. When you hurried towards God I followed you, indeed, I went first to take the veil – perhaps you were thinking how Lot's wife turned back when you made me put on the religious habit and take my vows before you gave yourself to God. Your lack of trust in me over this one thing, I confess, overwhelmed me with grief and shame. I would have had no hesitation, God knows, in following you or going ahead at your bidding to the flames of Hell. My heart was not in me but with you, and now, even more, if it is not with you it is nowhere; truly, without you it cannot exist. See that it fares well with you, I beg, as it will if it finds you kind, if you give grace in return for grace, small for great, words for deeds. If only your love had less confidence in me, my dear, so that you would be more concerned on my behalf! But as it is, the more I have made you feel secure in me, the more I have to bear with your neglect.

Remember, I implore you, what I have done, and think how much you owe me. While I enjoyed with you the pleasures of the flesh, many were uncertain whether I was prompted by love or lust; but now the end is proof of the beginning. I have finally denied myself every pleasure in obedience to your will, kept nothing for myself except to prove that now, even more, I am yours. Consider then your injustice, if when I deserve more you

[167]

give me less, or rather, nothing at all, especially when it is a small thing I ask of you and one you could so easily grant. And so, in the name of God to whom you have dedicated yourself, I beg you to restore your presence to me in the way you can – by writing me some word of comfort, so that in this at least I may find increased strength and readiness to serve God. When in the past you sought me out for sinful pleasures your letters came to me thick and fast, and your many songs put your Heloise on everyone's lips, so that every street and house echoed with my name. Is it not far better now to summon me to God than it was then to satisfy our lust? I beg you, think what you owe me, give ear to my pleas, and I will finish a long letter with a brief ending: farewell, my only love.

ABELARD to HELOISE

[Twelfth century]

To Heloise, his dearly beloved sister in Christ,
Abelard her brother in Christ.

If since our conversion from the world to God I have not yet written you any word of comfort or advice, it must not be attributed to indifference on my part but to your own good sense, in which I have always had such confidence that I did not think anything was needed; God's grace has bestowed on you all essentials to enable you to instruct the erring, comfort the weak and encourage the fainthearted, both by word and example, as, indeed, you have been doing since you first held the office of prioress under your abbess. So if you still watch over your daughters as carefully as you did previously over your sisters, it is sufficient to make me believe that any teaching or exhortation from me would now be wholly superfluous. If, on the other hand, in your humility you think differently, and you feel that you have need of my instruction and writings in matters pertaining to God, write to me what you want, so that I may answer as God permits me. Meanwhile thanks be to God who has filled all your hearts with anxiety for my desperate, unceasing perils, and made you share in my affliction; may divine mercy protect me through the support of your prayers and quickly crush Satan beneath our feet. To this end in particular, I hasten to send the psalter you earnestly begged from me, my sister once dear in the world and now dearest in Christ, so that you may offer a perpetual sacrifice of prayers to the Lord for our many great aberrations, and for the dangers which daily threaten me.

We have indeed many examples as evidence of the high position in the eyes of God and his saints which has been won by the prayers of the faithful, especially those of women on behalf of their dear ones and of wives for their husbands. The Apostle observes this closely when he bids us pray continually. We read that the Lord said to Moses 'Let me alone, to vent my anger upon them,' and to Jeremiah 'Therefore offer no prayer for these people nor stand in my path.' By these words the Lord himself makes it clear that the prayers of the devout set a kind of bridle on his wrath and check it from raging against sinners as fully as they deserve; just as a man who is willingly moved by his sense of justice to take vengeance can be turned aside by the entreaties of his friends and forcibly restrained, as it were, against his will. Thus when the Lord says to one who is praying or about to pray, 'Let me alone and do not stand in my path', he forbids prayers to be offered to him on behalf of the impious; yet the just man prays though the Lord forbids, obtains his requests and alters the sentence of the angry judge. And so the passage about Moses continues: 'And the Lord repented and spared his people the evil with which he had threatened them.' Elsewhere it is written about the universal works of God, 'He spoke, and it was.' But in this passage it is also recorded that he had said the people deserved affliction, but he had been prevented by the power of prayer from carrying out his words.

Consider then the great power of prayer, if we pray as we are bidden, seeing that the prophet won by prayer what he was forbidden to pray for, and turned God aside from his declared intention. And another prophet says to God: 'In thy wrath remember mercy.' The lords of the earth should listen and take note, for they are found obstinate rather than just in the execution of the justice they have decreed and pronounced; they blush to appear lax if they are merciful, and untruthful if they change a pronouncement or do not carry out a decision which lacked foresight, even if they can emend their words by their actions. Such men could properly be compared with Jephtha, who made a foolish vow and in carrying it out even more foolishly, killed his only daughter. But he who desires to be a 'member of his body' says with the Psalmist 'I will sing of mercy and justice unto thee, O Lord.' 'Mercy', it is written, 'exalts judgement,' in accordance with the threat elsewhere in the Scriptures: 'In that judgement there will be no mercy for the man who has shown no mercy.' The Psalmist himself considered this carefully when at the entreaty of the wife of Nabal the Carmelite, as an act of mercy he broke the oath he had justly sworn concerning her husband and the destruction of his house. Thus he set prayer above justice, and the man's wrongdoing was wiped out by the entreaties of his wife.

Here you have an example, sister, and an assurance how much your prayers for me may prevail on God, if this woman's did so much for her husband, seeing that God who is our father loves his children more than David did a suppliant woman. David was indeed considered a pious and merciful man, but God is piety and mercy itself. And the woman whose entreaties David heard then was an ordinary lay person, in no way bound to God by the profession of holy devotion; whereas if you alone are not enough to win an answer to your prayer, the holy convent of widows and virgins which is with you will succeed where you cannot by yourself. For when the Truth says to his disciples, 'When two or three have met together in my name, I am there among them,' and again, 'If two of you agree about any request you have to make, it shall be granted by my Father,' we can all see how the communal prayer of a holy congregation must prevail upon God. If, as the apostle James says, 'A good man's prayer is powerful and effective,' what should we hope for from the large numbers of a holy congregation? You know, dearest sister, from the thirty-eighth homily of St Gregory how much support the prayers of his fellow brethren quickly brought a brother, although he was unwilling and resisted. The depths of his misery, the fear of peril which tormented his unhappy soul, the utter despair and weariness of life which made him try to call his brethren from their prayers – all the details set out there cannot have escaped your understanding.

May this example give you and your convent of holy sisters greater confidence in prayer, so that I may be preserved alive for you all, through him, from whom, as Paul bears witness, women have even received back their dead raised to life. For if you turn the pages of the Old and New Testaments you will find that the greatest miracles of resurrection were shown only, or mostly, to women, and were performed for them or on them. The Old Testament records two instances of men raised from the dead at the entreaties of their mothers, by Elijah and his disciple Elisha. The Gospel, it is true, has three instances only of the dead being raised by the Lord but, as they were shown to women only, they provide factual confirmation of the Apostle's words I quoted above: 'Women received back their dead raised to life.' It was to a widow at the gate of the city of Nain that the Lord restored her son, moved by compassion for her, and he also raised Lazarus his own friend at the entreaty of his sisters Mary and Martha. And when he granted this same favour to the daughter of the ruler of the synagogue at her father's petition, again 'women received back their dead raised to life', for in being brought back to life she received her own body from death just as those other women received the bodies of their dead.

Now these resurrections were performed with only a few interceding; and so the multiplied prayers of your shared devotion should easily win the preservation of my own life. The more God is pleased by the abstinence and continence which women have dedicated to him, the more willing he will be to grant their prayers. Moreover, it may well be that the majority of those raised from the dead were not of the faith, for we do not read that the widow mentioned above whose son was raised without her asking was a believer. But in our case we are bound together by the integrity of our faith and united in our profession of the same religious life.

Let me now pass from the holy convent of your community, where so many virgins and widows are dedicated to continual service of the Lord, and come to you alone, you whose sanctity must surely have the greatest influence in the eyes of God, and who are bound to do everything possible on my behalf, especially now when I am in the toils of such adversity. Always remember then in your prayers him who is especially yours; watch and pray the more confidently as you recognize your cause is just, and so more acceptable to him to whom you pray. Listen, I beg you, with the ear of your heart to what you have so often heard with your bodily ear. In the book of Proverbs it is written that 'A capable wife is her husband's crown,' and again, 'Find a wife and you find a good thing; so you will earn the favour of the Lord'; yet again, 'Home and wealth may come down from ancestors; but an intelligent wife is a gift from from the Lord.' In Ecclesiasticus too it says that 'A good wife makes a happy husband,' and a little later, 'A good wife means a good life.' And we have it on the Apostle's authority that 'the unbelieving husband now belongs to God through his wife'. A special instance of this was granted by God's grace in our own country of France, when Clovis the king was converted to the Christian faith more by the prayers of his wife than by the preaching of holy men; his entire kingdom was then placed under divine law so that humbler men should be encouraged by the example of their betters to persevere in prayer. Indeed, such perseverance is warmly recommended to us in a parable of the Lord which says: 'If the man perseveres in his knocking, though he will not provide for him out of friendship, the very shamelessness of the request will make him get up and give him all he needs.' It was certainly by what I might call this shamelessness in prayer that Moses (as I said above) softened the harshness of divine justice and changed its sentence.

You know, beloved, the warmth of charity your convent once used to show me in their prayers at the times I could be with you.

At the conclusion of each of the Hours every day they would offer this special prayer to the Lord on my behalf; after the proper response and versicle were pronounced and sung they added prayers and a collect, as follows:

RESPONSE: Forsake me not, O Lord: Keep not far from me, my God.

VERSICLE: Make haste, O Lord, to help me.

PRAYER: Save thy servant, O my God, whose hope is in thee; Lord hear my prayer, and let my cry for help reach thee.

(LET US PRAY) O God, who through thy servant hast been pleased to gather together thy handmaidens in thy name, we beseech thee to grant both to him and to us that we persevere in thy will. Through our Lord, etc.

But now that I am not with you, there is all the more need for the support of your prayers, the more I am gripped by fear of greater peril. And so I ask of you in entreaty, and entreat you in asking, particularly now that I am absent from you, to show me how truly your charity extends to the absent by adding this form of special prayer at the conclusion of each hour:

RESPONSE: O Lord, Father and Ruler of my life, do not desert me, lest I fall before my adversaries and my enemy gloats over me.

VERSICLE: Grasp shield and buckler and rise up to help me, lest my enemy gloats.

PRAYER: Save thy servant, O my God, whose hope is in thee. Send him help, O Lord, from thy holy place, and watch over him from Zion. Be a tower of strength to him, O Lord, in the face of his enemy. Lord hear my prayer, and let my cry for help reach thee.

(LET US PRAY) O God who through thy servant hast been pleased to gather together thy handmaidens in thy name, we beseech thee to protect him in all adversity and restore him in safety to thy handmaidens. Through our Lord, etc.

But if the Lord shall deliver me into the hands of my enemies so that they overcome and kill me, or by whatever chance I enter upon the way of all flesh while absent from you, wherever my body may lie, buried or unburied, I beg you to have it brought to your burial-ground, where our daughters, or rather, our sisters in Christ may see my tomb more often and thereby be encouraged to pour out their prayers more fully to the Lord on my behalf. There is no place, I think, so safe and salutary for a soul grieving for its sins and desolated by its transgressions than that which is specially consecrated to the true Paraclete, the Comforter, and which is particularly designated for his name. Nor do I believe that there is any place more fitting for Christian burial among the faithful than one amongst women dedicated to Christ. Women were concerned for the tomb of our Lord Jesus Christ, they came ahead and followed after, bringing precious ointments, keeping close watch around this tomb, weeping for the death of the Bridegroom, as it is written: 'The women sitting at the tomb wept and lamented for the Lord.' And there they were first reassured about his resurrection by the appearance of an angel and the words he spoke to them; later on they were found worthy both to taste the joy of his resurrection when he twice appeared to them, and also to touch him with their hands.

Finally, I ask this of you above all else: at present you are over-anxious about the danger to my body, but then your chief concern must be for the salvation of my soul, and you must show the dead man how much you loved the living by the special support of prayers chosen for him.

Live, fare you well, yourself and your sisters with you,

Live, but I pray, in Christ be mindful of me.

HELOISE to ABELARD

[Twelfth century]

To her only one after Christ, she who is his alone in Christ.

I am surprised, my only love, that contrary to custom in letter-writing and, indeed, to the natural order, you have thought fit to put my name before yours in the greeting which heads your letter, so that we have woman before man, wife before husband, handmaid before master, nun before monk, deaconess before priest and abbess before abbot. Surely the right and proper order is for those who write to their superiors or equals to put their names before their own, but in letters to inferiors, precedence in order of address follows precedence in rank.

We were also greatly surprised when instead of bringing us the healing balm of comfort you increased our desolatiòn and made the tears to flow which you should have dried. For which of us could remain dry-eyed on hearing the words you wrote towards the end of your letter: 'But if the Lord shall deliver me into the hands of my enemies so that they overcome and kill me . . .'? My dearest, how could you think such a thought? How could you give voice to it? Never may God be so forgetful of his humble handmaids as to let them outlive you; never may he grant us a life which would be harder to bear than any form of death. The proper course would be for you to perform our funeral rites, for you to commend our souls to God, and to send ahead of you those whom you assembled for God's service – so that you need no longer be troubled by worries for us, and follow after us the more gladly because freed from concern for our salvation. Spare us, I implore you, master, spare us words such as these which can only intensify our existing unhappiness; do not deny us, before death, the one thing by which we live. 'Each day has trouble enough of its own,' and that day, shrouded in bitterness, will bring with it distress enough to all it comes upon. 'Why is it necessary,' says Seneca, 'to summon evil' and to destroy life before death comes?

You ask us, my love, if you chance to die when absent from us, to have your body brought to our burial-ground so that you may reap a fuller harvest from the prayers we shall offer in constant memory of you. But how could you supppose that our memory of you could ever fade? Besides, what time will there be then which will be fitting for prayer, when extreme distress will allow us no peace, when the soul will lose its power of reason and the tongue its use of speech? Or when the frantic mind, far from being resigned, may even (if I may say so) rage against God himself, and provoke him with complaints instead of placating him with prayers? In our misery then we shall have time only for tears and no power to pray; we shall be hurrying to follow, not to bury you, so that we may share your grave instead of laying you in it. If we lose our life in you, we shall not be able to go on living when you leave us, I would not even have us live to see that day, for if the mere mention of your death is death for us, what will the reality be if it finds us still alive? God grant we may never live on to perform this duty, to render you the service which we look for from you alone; in this may we go before, not after you!

And so, I beg you, spare us – spare her at least, who is yours alone, by refraining from words like these. They pierce our hearts with swords of death, so that what comes before is more painful than death itself. A heart which is exhausted with grief cannot find peace, nor can a mind preoccupied with anxieties genuinely devote itself to God. I beseech you not to hinder God's service to which you specially committed us. Whatever has to come to us bringing with it total grief we must hope will come suddenly, without torturing us far in advance with useless apprehension which no foresight can relieve. This is what the poet has in mind when he prays to God:

> May it be sudden, whatever you plan for us; may man's mind
> Be blind to the future. Let him hope on in his fears.*

But if I lose you, what is left for me to hope for? What reason for continuing on life's pilgrimage, for which I have no support but you, and none in you save the knowledge that you are alive, now that I am forbidden all other pleasures in you and denied even the joy of your presence which from time to time could restore me to myself? O God – if I dare say it – cruel to me in everything! O merciless mercy! O Fortune who is only ill-fortune, who has already spent on me so many of the shafts she uses in her battle against mankind that she has none left with which to vent her

*Lucan, *Pharsalia II*, 14–15.

anger on others. She has emptied a full quiver on me, so that henceforth no one else need fear her onslaughts, and if she still had a single arrow she could find no place in me to take a wound. Her only dread is that through my many wounds death may end my sufferings; and though she does not cease to destroy me, she still fears the destruction which she hurries on.

Of all wretched women I am the most wretched, and amongst the unhappy I am unhappiest. The higher I was exalted when you preferred me to all other women, the greater my suffering over my own fall and yours, when I was flung down; for the higher the ascent, the heavier the fall. Has Fortune ever set any great or noble woman above me or made her my equal, only to be similarly cast down and crushed with grief? What glory she gave me in you, what ruin she brought upon me through you! Violent in either extreme, she showed no moderation in good or evil. To make me the saddest of all women she first made me blessed above all, so that when I thought how much I had lost, my consuming grief would match my crushing loss, and my sorrow for what was taken from me would be the greater for the fuller joy of possession which had gone before; and so that the happiness of supreme ecstasy would end in the supreme bitterness of sorrow.

(DORA) CARRINGTON to LYTTON STRACHEY

Saturday morning, 12 o'ck [14 May, 1921]
The Mill House, Tidmarsh

My dearest Lytton, There is a great deal to say and I feel very incompetent to write it today. Last night I composed a great many letters to you, almost till three in the morning. I then wrote an imaginary letter and bared my very soul to you. This morning I don't feel so intimate. *You* mayn't value my pent up feelings and a tearful letter. *I* rather object to them not being properly received and left about. Well there was more of a crisis than I thought when I wrote to you on Thursday. Ralph had one of his break downs and completely collapsed. He threw himself in the Woolves' arms and asked their sympathy and advice. Leonard and Virginia both said it was hopeless for him to go on as he was, that he must either marry me, or leave me completely. He came down to Reading yesterday and met me at the Coffee tea shop. He looked dreadfully ill and his mouth twitched. I'd really made my mind up some time ago that if it came to the ultimate point, I would give in. Only typically I preferred to defer it indefinitely and avoid it if possible. You see I knew there was nothing really to hope for from you – Well ever since the beginning. Then Alix told me last spring what you told James. That you were slightly terrified of my becoming dependent on you, and a permanent limpet and other things. I didn't tell you, because after all, it is no use having scenes. But you must know Ralph repeated every word you once told him in bed; that night when we were all three together. The next day we went for a walk on the Swindon downs. Perhaps you remember. I shall never forget that spot of ground, just outside Chisledon, at the foot of the downs, when he repeated every word you had said. He told me of course because he was jealous and wanted to hurt me. But it altered things, because ever after that I had a terror of being physically on your nerves and revolting you. I never came again to your bedroom. Why am I raking all this up now? Only to tell you that all these years I have known all along that my life with you was limited. I could never hope for it to become permanent. After all Lytton, you are the only person who I have ever had an all absorbing passion for. I shall never have another. I couldn't now. I had one of the most self abasing loves that a person can have. You could throw me into transports of happiness and dash me into deluges of tears and despair, all by a few words. But these aren't reproaches. For after all it's getting on for 6 years since I first met you at Asheham; and that's a long time to be happy. And I know we shall always be friends now until I die. Of course these years of Tidmarsh when we were quite alone will always be the happiest I ever spent. And I've such a store of good things which I've saved up, that I feel I could never be lonely again now. Still it's too much of a strain to be quite alone here waiting to see you or craning my nose and eyes out of the top window at 41 Gordon Square to see if you are coming down the street, when I know we'll be better friends, if you aren't haunted by the idea that I am sitting depressed in some corner of the world waiting for your footstep. It's slightly mythical of course. I can pull myself together if I want to and I am more aware than you think, the moment I am getting on your nerves and when I am not wanted. I saw the relief you felt at Ralph taking me away, so to speak, off your hands. I think he'll make me happier, than I should be entirely by myself and it certainly prevents me becoming morbid about you. And as Ralph said last night you'll never leave us. Because in spite of our dullnesses, nobody loves you nearly as much as we do. So in the café in that vile city of Reading, I said I'd marry him. And now he's written to his father and told him. After all I don't believe it will make much difference and to see him so happy is a rather definite thing. I'd probably never marry anyone else and I doubt if a kinder creature exists on this earth. Last night in bed he told me everything Virginia and Leonard had told him. Again a conversation you had with them was repeated to me. Ralph was so happy he didn't hear me gasp and as it was dark he didn't see the tears run down my cheeks. Virginia told him that you had told them you didn't intend to come to Tidmarsh much after Italy and you were nervous lest I'd feel I had a sort of claim on you if I lived with [you] for a long time, ten years and that they all wondered how you could have stood me so long and how on earth we lived together alone here, as I didn't understand a word of literature and we had nothing in common intellectually or physically. That was wrong. For nobody I think could have loved the Ballades, Donne, and Macaulay's Essays and best of all, Lytton's Essays, as much as I. Virginia then told him that she thought I was still in love with you. Ralph asked me if I was. I said I didn't think perhaps I was as much as I used to be. So now I shall never tell *you* I do care again. It goes after today somewhere deep down inside me and I'll not resurrect it to hurt either, you, or Ralph. Never again. He knows I am not in love with him. But he feels my affections are great enough to make him happy if I live with him. I cried last night Lytton, whilst he slept by my side sleeping happily. I cried to think of a savage cynical fate which had made it impossible for my love ever to be used by you. You never knew, or never will know the very big and devastating love I had for you. How I adored every hair, every curl on your beard. How I devoured you whilst you read to me at night. How I loved the smell of your face in your sponge. Then the ivory skin on your hands, your voice, and your hat when I saw it coming along the top of the garden wall from my window. Say you will remember it, that it wasn't all lost and that you'll forgive me for this out burst, and always be my friend. Just thinking of you now makes me cry so I can't see this paper, and yet so happy that the next moment I am calm. I shall be with you in Italy in two weeks, how lovely that will be. And this summer we shall all be very happy together. Please never show this letter to anyone. Ralph is such a dear, I don't feel I'll ever regret marrying him. Though I never will change my maiden name that I have kept for so long – so you mayn't ever call me anything but Carrington. . . .

LYTTON STRACHEY to (DORA) CARRINGTON

[20 May 1921]
. . . But I hope that in any case you never doubted my love for you. Do you know how difficult I find it to express my feelings in letters or talk? It is sometimes terrible – and I don't understand why it should be so; and sometimes it seems to me that you underrate what I feel. You realise that I have varying moods, but my fundamental feelings you perhaps don't realise so well. Probably it is my fault. It is perhaps much easier to show one's peevishness than one's affection and admiration! Oh my dear, do you really want me to tell you that I 'love you as a friend' ? – But of course that is absurd, and you *do* know very well that I love you

as something more than a friend, you angelic creature, whose goodness to me has made me happy for years, and whose presence in my life has been, and always will be, one of the most important things in it. Your letter made me cry, I feel a poor old miserable creature, and I may have brought more unhappiness to you than anything else. I only pray that it is not so, and that my love for you, even though it is not what you desire, may yet make our relationship a blessing to you – as it has been to me. Remember that I too have never had my moon! We are all helpless in these things – dreadfully helpless. I am lonely and I am all too truly growing old, and if there was a chance that your decision meant that I should somehow or other lose you, I don't think I could bear it. You and Ralph and our life at Tidmarsh are what I care for most in the world – almost (apart from my work and some few people) the *only* things I care for . . .

. . . you seemed in your letter to suggest that my love for you has diminished as time has gone on: that is not so. I am sure that it has increased. It is true that the first excitement, which I always (and I suppose most people) have at the beginning of an affair, has gone off: but something much deeper has grown up instead.

MARY WOLLSTONECRAFT to GILBERT IMLAY

Paris, 1794
Evening, September 23

I have been playing and laughing with the little girl so long, that I cannot take up my pen to address you without emotion. Pressing her to my bosom, she looked so like you (entre nous, your best looks, for I do not admire your commercial face), every nerve seemed to vibrate to the touch, and I began to think that there was something in the assertion of man and wife being one – for you seemed to pervade my whole frame, quickening the beat of my heart, and lending me the sympathetic tears you excited.

Have I anything more to say to you? No; not for the present – the rest is all flown away; and indulging tenderness for you, I cannot now complain of some people here, who have ruffled my temper for two or three days past.

Zelda Fitzgerald to F. Scott Fitzgerald

[1920]

I look down the tracks and see you coming – and out of every haze & mist your darling rumpled trousers are hurrying to me – Without you, dearest dearest I couldn't see or hear or feel or think – or live – I love you so and I'm never in all our lives going to let us be apart another night. It's like begging for mercy of a storm or killing Beauty or growing old, without you. I want to kiss you so – and in the back where your dear hair starts and your chest – I love you – and I can't tell you how much – To think that I'll *die* without your knowing – Goofo, you've *got* to try [to] feel how much I do – how inanimate I am when you're gone – I can't even hate these damnable people – Nobodys got any right to live but us – and they're dirtying up our world and I can't hate them because I want you so – Come Quick – Come Quick to me – I could never do without you if you hated me and were covered with sores like a leper – if you ran away with another woman and starved me and beat me – I still would want you *I know*—

Lover, Lover, Darling –
Your Wife

DOROTHY THOMPSON to SINCLAIR LEWIS

[1942]

I cannot recall that you ever asked me what I would like, even in the years that we lived together. But what I do not like is a divorce, and I am not going to get one. I know the divorce laws of Vermont, for at one time, I confess, I thought of getting a divorce. It was because of the brutally inconsiderate manner of your treatment of our relationship in your affair with Marcella, even going so far as to introduce her to Wells as his future 'stepmother.' That filled me with blind rage, and I thought I should spare myself any future insults of this kind. But the very basis of my relationship to you is that I cannot cherish any grudge or feel even normal resentment against you that endures, or that changes my feelings. 'This is the way he is,' is the only answer I can find. . . .

Hundreds of times, Hal, you made me promise that I would never leave you and never divorce you. I made the promise, because I meant it, and felt so, also. Why should I believe that you meant that and mean this, or that you did not know your own mind then and do know it now? I have never been able to repudiate our marriage, even to myself. Now you ask me to do it publicly. Such a step would be an unbearable self-violation. . . . In a curious way you are asking me to make something between us mutual again – to make common an aversion as once you besought me to make common a love. But I cannot. It is *not* common. The whole case would be an unmitigated fraud. It would not make me free. I shall live with you, in one sense, to the end of my life. . . . Don't you see, Hal, that you are asking *me* to banish *your* resentment? And you ask me, by attempting to blackmail me through the child, knowing how deeply I wish him to have a father. But your relationship to Michael depends upon your feelings for Michael, and nothing *I* do will influence those feelings. Only what you do will influence them. Either you care for him, or you don't. My getting a divorce will not awaken a love in your heart for our child, if it is not there. . . . I still live every day in the crazy illusion that the door will open and you will come back – as though from Bermuda. I know with my merciless intellect that you will not come home, but there are realms outside intelligence and outside logic.

ABOUT
LETTERS

11 November, 1912

Fräulein Felice!

I am now going to ask you a favor which sounds quite crazy, and which I should regard as such, were I the one to receive the letter. It is also the very greatest test that even the kindest person could be put to. Well, this is it:

Write to me only once a week, so that your letter arrives on Sunday – for I cannot endure your daily letters, I am incapable of enduring them. For instance, I answer one of your letters, then lie in bed in apparent calm, but my heart beats through my entire body and is conscious only of you. I belong to you; there is really no other way of expressing it, and that is not strong enough. But for this very reason I don't want to know what you are wearing; it confuses me so much that I cannot deal with life; and that's why I don't want to know that you are fond of me. If I did, how could I, fool that I am, go on sitting in my office, or here at home, instead of leaping onto a train with my eyes shut and opening them only when I am with you? Oh, there is a sad, sad reason for not doing so. To make it short: My health is only just good enough for myself alone, not good enough for marriage, let alone fatherhood. Yet when I read your letter, I feel I could overlook even what cannot possibly be overlooked.

If only I had your answer now! And how horribly I torment you, and how I compel you, in the stillness of your room, to read this letter, as nasty a letter as has ever lain on your desk! Honestly, it strikes me sometimes that I prey like a spectre on your felicitous name! If only I had mailed Saturday's letter, in which I implored you never to write to me again, and in which I gave a similar promise. Oh God, what prevented me from sending that letter? All would be well. But is a peaceful solution possible now? Would it help if we wrote to each other only once a week? No, if my suffering could be cured by such means it would not be serious. And already I foresee that I shan't be able to endure even the Sunday letters. And so, to compensate for Saturday's lost opportunity, I ask you with what energy remains to me at the end of this letter: If we value our lives, let us abandon it all.

Did I think of signing myself *Dein*? No, nothing could be more false. No, I am forever fettered to myself, that's what I am, and that's what I must try to live with.

Franz

FRANZ KAFKA to FELICE BAUER

19 November, 1912

Dearest, this is not a reproach, simply a request for an explanation; I am getting very depressed because I am completely at sea. It is quite right that we should stop this madness of so many letters; yesterday I even started a letter on this subject which I will send tomorrow; but surely we must be in complete agreement about the change in our writing habits; it must be discussed, and announced in advance; otherwise one would go crazy. Well then, how can I explain the fact that, according to your own information, you received or at any rate knew about my last registered letter on Friday morning, but didn't answer it till Saturday; that in Saturday's letter you said you would write again that day, but didn't; that on Monday, instead of getting the two promised letters, I get none; that during the whole of Sunday you wrote not a single word, not until late that night, when you wrote the letter which of course made me happy, insofar as I am still capable of being happy, and you didn't write even on

Monday, wouldn't have written at all if I hadn't sent that telegram, since the only letter I received, dated Monday, is the express letter. But the strangest and most frightening thing is this: You are ill for a day and a half, yet attend rehearsals every day of the week; despite your illness, you go dancing on Saturday night, come home at 7 in the morning, stay up till 1 the next, and on Monday you go to a private dance. For heaven's sake, what sort of life is that! Dearest, explanations please! Forget about the flowers and books. They are simply a sign of my helplessness.

Franz

On a separate page, enclosed:
I now see that in your Sunday letter you again promised definitely to write on Monday.

FRANZ KAFKA to FELICE BAUER

20 November, 1912

Dearest, what have I done that makes you torment me so? No letter again today, neither by the first mail nor the second. You do make me suffer! While one written word from you could make me happy! You've had enough of me; there is no other explanation, it's not surprising after all; what is incomprehensible, though, is that you don't write and tell me so. If I am to go on living at all, I cannot go on vainly waiting for news of you, as I have done these last few interminable days. But I no longer have any hope of hearing from you. I shall have to repeat specifically the farewell you bid me in silence. I should like to throw myself bodily on this letter, so that it cannot be mailed, but it must be mailed. I shall expect no further letters.

Franz

[Probably night of November 20 to 21, 1912]
Dearest, my dearest, it is 1:30 at night. Have I offended you

with this morning's letter? How am I to know about the responsibilities you have toward your relatives and friends! You take all that trouble and I trouble you with my reproaches about your troubles. Please, dearest, forgive me! Send me a rose to show that you have forgiven. I am not actually tired, but numb and heavy, and can't find the right words. All I can say is: Stay with me, don't leave me. And should one of my enemies from within write to you as he did this morning, don't believe him, just ignore him and look straight into my heart. Life indeed is so hard and sad, how can one hope to hold anyone with nothing but written words? To hold is what hands are for. But this hand of mine has held your hand, which has become indispensable to my life, for only three moments: when I entered the room, when you promised me the trip to Palestine, and when I, fool that I am, allowed you to get into the elevator.

May I kiss you then? On this miserable paper? I might as well open the window and kiss the night air.

Dearest, don't be angry with me! That's all I ask of you.

Franz

FRANK HARRIS to RITA (ERIKA LORENZ)

[1927]

I went in today to the Express Co. and got your wire. Straightway the clouds lifted, the sun shone and my heart came into my mouth: I was myself again: but you mustn't do this Rita, it's wrong of you, and one of these days, you'll be sorry for it. Love, as I told you is a plant of tenderest growth: treat it well, take thought for it and it may grow strong and perfume your whole life. But treat it carelessly, leave it a whole week without a word and suddenly when you want it, you'll not find it. I've had four dreadful days: when you did not write, I turned again to my work, and lost my loneliness in labor; but even now I can't forgive you entirely: I had put you on a pedestal – high above ordinary woman: but now I'm no longer so sure of you. Yes, you've big ... passion in you and a love of truth; but you can't love me as I thought you did, or you would not have left me 8 days without a word. There's something in you I don't understand and cannot make out. .... There are some men that neglect or coldness seem to excite; but I have always been made much of, always had the desire of perfection in me – in my work and my life. I was so proud of you and your self-sacrificing devotion; but now you've made me doubt. Quick, quick, I want your explanation and can only pray it may be completely satisfying. Already I excuse you: you are so young and you push me from you: you will not give yourself completely to me – you child! But Rita mine, you must never make me suffer as I've suffered in this last week: I'm too proud, too old to endure it. I've made all sorts of blunders in these 8 days: I've offended old and tried friends, could not listen to them or show interest in their troubles; I was wounded to the soul, what did their petty troubles matter to me wounded to the soul. No letter yet. Wednesday 14th. None since 4th!!!!!! Mean child.

NAPOLEON BONAPARTE to JOSEPHINE BONAPARTE

Verona, 3 Frimaire, year V [1797]

To Josephine, in Milan

I love you no longer; on the contrary, I detest you. You are a wretch, truly perverse, truly stupid, a real Cinderella. You never write to me at all, you do not love your husband; you know the pleasure that your letters give him yet you cannot even manage to write him half a dozen lines, dashed off in a moment!

What then do you do all day, Madame? What business is so vital that it robs you of the time to write to your faithful lover? What attachment can be stifling and pushing aside the love, the tender and constant love which you promised him? Who can this wonderful new lover be who takes up your every moment, rules your days and prevents you from devoting your attention to your husband? Beware, Josephine; one fine night the doors will be broken down and there I shall be.

In truth, I am worried, my love, to have no news from you; write me a four-page letter instantly made up from those delightful words which fill my heart with emotion and joy.

I hope to hold you in my arms before long, when I shall lavish upon you a million kisses, burning as the equatorial sun.

Bonaparte

From the *Pillow Book of Sei Shonagon*

[Tenth century]

On one occasion a man, who invariably sent me a letter after we had spent the night together, declared that he saw no point in our relationship and that he had nothing more to say to me. There was no word from him on the next day. 'When dawn appeared' without the usual next-morning letter, I could not help feeling rather gloomy. 'Well,' I thought as the day advanced, 'he really meant what he says.'

It rained very hard on the day after that. Noon came and still I had heard nothing from him: obviously he had forgotten all about me. Then in the evening, while I was sitting on the edge of the veranda, a child arrived with an open umbrella in one hand and a letter in the other. I opened the letter and read it with more than usual haste. 'The rain that swells the water' was the message, and I found this more charming than if he had sent me a whole sheaf of poems.

Dorothy Osborne to William Temple

[6 March 1653?]

Sir,

Your last letter came like a pardon to one upon the block. I have given over the hopes on't, having received my letters by the other carrier, who uses always to be last. The loss put me hugely out of order, and you would both have pitied and laughed at me if you could have seen how woodenly I entertained the widow, who came hither the day before, and surprised me very much. Not being able to say anything, I got her to cards, and there with a great deal of patience lost my money to her – or rather I gave it as my ransom. In the midst of our play, in comes my blessed boy with your letter, and, in earnest, I was not able to disguise the joy it gave me, though one was by that is not much your friend, and took notice of a blush that for my life I could not keep back. I put up the letter in my pocket, and made what haste I could to lose the money I had left, that I might take occasion to go fetch some more; but I did not make such haste back again, I can assure you. I took time enough to have coined myself some money if I had had the art on't, and left my brother enough to make all his addresses to her if he were so disposed. I know not whether he was pleased or not, but I am sure I was. . . .

Serenos to Isisdora

[Second century, Roman]

Serenos to Isisdora, his Sister and Lady, very many greetings. Before all else I pray for your health, and daily and nightly make supplication before Thoeris who loves you. I want you to know that ever since you left me I've been in mourning, weeping by day and lamenting by day. Since I bathed with you on Phaophi 12 I didn't bathe or anoint myself till Hathur 12. You have sent me letters that could move a stone, so much have your words stirred me. On the very instant I wrote you an answer and delivered it on the 12th sealed up along with your letters. Apart from what you say and write, 'But Colobos has made me a whore,' he said to me, 'Your wife sent me word to say, "He's sold the chain and himself he put me in the boat."' Do you say these things so that I won't be trusted any longer about what I put aboard? Look how often I've sent for you. Do let me know if you're coming or not.

STENDHAL to MADAME CURIAL

Florence, 20 July 1819

Madame, perhaps, disgraced as I am, it may strike you as unseemly that I should have the temerity to write. If I have made myself hateful to you by doing so, I shall at least attempt not to compound my ill-fortune, and therefore beseech you to tear up my letter without reading further.

If on the other hand your sensitive though over-proud spirit should have the goodness to treat me as an unhappy friend, and if you should condescend to send me news of yourself, I beg you to write to me at Bologna, where I am compelled to travel: 'Al Signor Beyle, nella locanda dell'Aquila Nera.' I am truly anxious about your health. If you were ill, would you be so cruel as not to inform me in a note? But I must be prepared for all eventualities. Happy is the heart which is warmed by the calm, discreet and steady light of a feebly burning lamp! It is said that such a heart loves and that it commits no improprieties which are harmful to itself or to others. But the heart which blazes with volcanic fires cannot please the object of its devotion, acts extravagantly, lacks tact and eventually burns itself out. I am deeply unhappy.

Henri

DENIS DIDEROT to SOPHIE VOLLAND

Paris, 14 July 1762

How is it that I have just received your seventh letter when you have only had four of the nine I have written you, including this one? But let us not worry about the speed of the post; it will never go as fast as we want. Passionate lovers would like the whole world to run according to their wishes.

What a lot of things I have to tell you, some of them happy and others sad. My letters are a more or less faithful history of my life. Without meaning to, I am doing what I have so often wished for. Why, I said, an astronomer will spend thirty years of his life on top of an observatory, his eye glued day and night to the end of a telescope, simply to determine the movement of a star, and no one makes a study of himself, no one has the courage to keep an accurate record of all the thoughts that come into his mind, all the feelings that agitate his heart, all his sorrows and joys. In this way century after century will go past without anyone knowing whether life is a good or a bad thing, whether human nature is good or evil, and what makes up happiness and unhappiness. But it would need a lot of courage to reveal everything. One might find it easier to accuse oneself of planning a great crime than to admit harbouring petty or low or despicable feelings. It might be less difficult to write in one's confessions: 'I desired the throne at the expense of its present occupier's life', than to write: 'One day when I was at the baths among a crowd of young men, I noticed a youth of unusual beauty and I could not prevent myself from going close to him.' This sort of self-analysis would have its uses for the writer too. I am sure that in the long run one would be anxious to have nothing but good things to enter in the record each evening. But what about you, would you reveal everything? Try asking Uranie the same question, for there is absolutely no point in committing yourself to a plan of sincerity which frightens you. As for me, far away from you as I am, there is nothing which brings me closer to you than to tell you everything and by my words to make you a spectator of my life. I don't know whether you won't already find something like this in some of my letters – and perhaps something too of what I am about to write. But what of it!

I promised you foolish things and serious things. Here are the foolish ones to start with. Madame d'Houdetot, who has innumerable hobby-horses of every shape and size, had bored her husband to distraction with her chatter about painting, sculpture, music, poetry, eloquence, love, solitude, the countryside, and all the other things with which she surrounds herself so as to be always happy and excited. Note that the husband only likes horses and gambling, which, as you can imagine, had not been mentioned once. In his annoyance he waits until the flood has subsided, gets up and says: 'Personally, I have no taste, thank God.' And she comes back at him immediately: 'Personally, I have every taste there is, thank God.' What do you think of that?

Some time ago now, I can't remember if it was in town or in the country, I heard her saying at supper: 'Every moment of the day I acquire some new taste, and I never lose a single one.' I was still in the drawing-room with Madame d'Holbach and I said to her apropos of the countess's innumerable tastes: 'Upon my word, I would prefer one solid one.' 'So would I', said the Baroness.

When I have dinner on the island, which is not as often as I am asked, we sometimes amuse ourselves playing draughts. One day not long ago I was having a game with Damilaville. There was a good move he could make, but he didn't notice it and his lady friend gave him a push with her foot to make him see it. But instead of making use of her advice, he deliberately made a wrong move and said quite sharply to her: 'Don't push me, madam; I never make a move which is pointed out to me.' She was all shamefaced and assured me that this was the first time she had ever done anything of the kind, but I maliciously said that I didn't believe a word of it and that I was very pleased to learn why I had lost so many games, at which she burst into tears. I didn't want a trivial matter like this to take such a serious turn. The husband and the lover went off. I stayed with her and tried to calm her silly head, but it wasn't an easy business. According to her,

Damilaville had compromised her and made her look ridiculous and this little kick, which she described as a terrible fault, would ruin her in my eyes. The only way I could find of comforting her a little was to swear that if it had been me sitting next to the woman I loved, it would have happened not once but a hundred times. 'Do you really mean it?' 'Really.' 'You are only saying that to console me.' And so to stop her tears I launched into a series of lies, for I know quite well that if I saw Sophie about to lose a fortune by playing the wrong card, I would do nothing to stop her. What folly to want even Chance to favour the one you love, and to want him to beat everyone else at dice, cards, or roulette! If such little successes improve our opinion of a man, it follows that an insignificant loss will lower him slightly in our esteem. I should not be sorry to appear incompetent or even ridiculous in certain trivial matters. Woe to the woman who wants her lover to be a prodigy in every way!

So you think that I really love you? And what makes you think this, pray? Have I lived my life beside you? Have you seen me devoting myself entirely to your happiness? Have I nursed you when you were ill, comforted you when you were unhappy, helped you when you were poor? Have I envied all those about you the privilege of doing your hair, dressing you, and serving you? Do you know the hundredth part of my passion for you? Only I know how much I love you. You do not know it and never will. It seems to me that my feelings are proof against all the trials of life. Yes, my heart I am satisfied with, but all the rest is pitiful, extremely pitiful. How glad I am that you do not know your own value, and all that a lover like me is capable of doing. Oh my dear, love and friendship are not the same for me as they are for other men. When once I have said in my heart: 'I am her lover, I am her friend', you might well be alarmed if I told you all that goes with this. This is how I see it, my dear: either love and friendship are worthless, or else they will make us follow the one we love to the final ordeal, and even on to the. . . . No, you of little soul, I will not finish; I do not want to make you shudder. Love, friendship, and religion are the source of the most violent passions in life.

In one of my recent letters you will find a conversation between Madame Duclos and me. I could not get it out of my head for several days, and I cannot tell you the ideas it gave me. Others might think them odd, but Uranie and you will be able to see the truth in them. I have been thinking that a man whose behaviour when wealthy was as sublime as I imagine Damilaville's would be, might be afraid that he would demean himself if he continued to seek the pleasures of love. He would fear that people might attribute his noble actions to this single petty motive. If ever he returned to his mistress's arms, it would be very infrequently and in special circumstances which excused everything. Thus one day he might be sitting with his love, they might recall the beginnings of their friendship, and their hearts would beat faster, they would look tenderly at one another and press one another's hands, kisses would be given and returned, a few tears would be shed, and it might end in a sweet moment of weakness. Do you imagine that a charming girl's benefactor who has any sort of delicacy dares speak to her of gallantry and love? If he did, what sort of name should we give to his kindness? And how could she accept it?

Here's another thing – for when I write to you, I talk as if I were by your side, with one arm on the back of your chair, chatting to you. There is no order or plan or logic in what I write; I put down everything that happens both inside and outside the space occupied by my life, both where I am and where others move about me, both where I feel constantly that I love you to distraction, and where everyone else torments themselves for a thousand and one silly trifles. So conscience is never totally depraved? Does there always come a time then when unhappiness awakens remorse in us? Come then, brigands and villains, come and listen to one of your troop on the brink of the precipice where his vices have led him, and where shame and despair await you. It is Gaudet I am thinking of as I write this. How cruelly clear his faults were to him, my dear! But unfortunately continuing adversity, though it make the virtuous man tire of doing good, never brings the evildoer back to virtue. Let a fierce animal out of the trap where it is caught, and it will do its best to devour you.

I have come to an arrangement with my publishers. I find my work less of a burden now that I am spurred on by the hope of getting together a dowry for my daughter. Previously her mother loved luxury enough for two. . . . But it's no good going on with that story. The audience to whom you have destined my letters will make me watch my step, because I shall no longer be talking to you alone, and the letters will be none the worse for that. I shall give praise more readily and be slower to criticize.

The sale of my library is still undecided. Pissot, my bookseller, has valued it at sixteen thousand one hundred and eighty-five francs, less the price of a few books which the buyers asked me for and which the bookseller is supplying.

Grimm is in a wretched state. He is concealing his unhappiness deep in his heart. He is losing his health. He is definitely going blind. I wrote to him today. What a letter it was, my love! In it you would have seen a true friend, depicted with those vivid, moving and delicate touches by which you were once so happy to recognize your lover. Immediately afterwards he arrived from La Briche. How glad we were to embrace one another! I kissed those eyes, and do not be jealous that I kissed them over and over as if they had been yours, those beautiful eyes where once I used to see the transparency of the sky, and which are doomed to darkness now. Would you believe it, that I had summoned him from La Briche to make him unhappy? I'll tell you why. Your affection makes you interested in everything that concerns me. Whatever I tell you about, I am always opening my heart to you and you can always see my passion hidden in some corner.

Last Sunday, I went to dinner at the Baron's, where I hadn't shown my face for more than a fortnight. There were seventeen or eighteen of us at table, but by half-past six I was left alone with the Baron, as often happens. He reproached me with not going to see him and his reproaches affected me. There are moments when this man's heart sets up a powerful resonance in me. After dinner we got into his carriage and went for a drive on the Petit Cours. He looked worried. Just imagine that some fellow, whom I shall call either a busybody or a villain when I know who it was, had taken it into his head to inform him that Madame d'Épinay was giving Grimm a terrible time and that she suspected Madame d'Holbach of stealing her lover, and her lover of seducing his friend's wife. No sooner had his suspicions been aroused than the Baron went off to ask his wife for more details. The Baroness, whose conscience was quite clear, told him all she knew. She admitted that she had often seen Madame d'Épinay in a bad mood, that Grimm's friendly behaviour towards her had won him sour looks from his mistress, that Madame d'Épinay and Madame de Maux had made far from equivocal remarks to her, that she had taken no notice of them, but had still resented being insulted, that certain people must be very used to criminal behaviour to suspect others of it on such slight evidence, that now he knew the truth, even though she had not wanted to tell him, and that whatever he decided to do, she would go along with it. The Baron gave his wife and friend their due. As for Madame d'Épinay, he seems determined to break with her. He is particularly angry, and rightly so, at the way she confided her jealous thoughts to Madame de Maux. If this lady starts gossiping, just think what the enemies who are all around spying on us will say. It would be nothing if they were the people concerned, but they will build it up into a real crime in us, since they are so envious of our good reputation. Can't you just hear them: 'So that's how philosophers carry on', etc. etc. I had foreseen how upset Grimm would be to see this friendship break up, since he had brought them together and regarded the Baron's house as a pool where his mistress would be happy to bathe on her return from Geneva. I thought it was my duty to tell him what had happened. Now he knows everything. We have schemes for a reconciliation. Will we succeed or will we fail? With such vacillating characters it is impossible to tell. It is certain that the Baroness is deeply hurt. She, her husband and Suard have gone to Sannois, to see Madame d'Houdetot. The same road goes to La Briche. They will pass Madame d'Épinay's door. I asked Madame d'Holbach if they would not stop there for a rest. 'That is not what I intend', she answered stiffly.

In the rest of our conversation I was able to discuss freely with

Grimm his extremely familiar way of behaving with Madame d'Holbach. I did not hide from him that if Madame d'Épinay was anything like me, she would have had cause enough for alarm, that if she had been patient enough to say nothing about it, I admired her, but that in her place I would have broken the ice long ago and either forced him to change his ways or scratched out his two bad eyes. He is so serious and sensible. To him we are like so many little children. Believe me, my dear, if this man and Uranie ever meet, they will love one another and they will regard us with pity from morning till night; and I do not like being pitied. So we must not let them meet.

This is my life. What a series of troubles! And this poor Grimm, what will he gain by his common sense, his wonderful prudence, his caution, his heart which keeps such perfect time with his head, like the hand of a clock whose movement depends on the regular swing of a pendulum? Does the consciousness that our suffering is not deserved diminish it? They say it does; so be it.

The saints are even able to take joy in the tribulations which God inflicts on them. I advise you to acquire a tincture of this fanaticism. The more Morphyse makes you suffer, the more highly you will think of yourself.

Your abbot from Moncetz is the Father Cyprian of Collé's extravaganza. It fits exactly. He is a man totally without religion. He secretly thinks virtue ridiculous. He regards the rest of us, the virtuous, as so many dupes. I'd bet that if one day at table you said as much to him jokingly, he would not protest overmuch, particularly if you were cunning enough to hint that you too were rather inclined to think the same way.

I really must call at the Rue des Vieux-Augustins one of these mornings. But it is time for dinner now. They are calling me to come. For the last two hours I have been in my workshop at Le Breton's writing you this long and tedious epistle which you will have quite a job deciphering. Just skip everything which makes you rub your spectacles on your sleeve. All that matters is these last few words: I count on your love, and my love will last as long as my life. The rest is meaningless. Goodbye, my dear. When are you expecting your sister?

VANESSA (ESTHER VANHOMRIGH) to JONATHAN SWIFT

[c. 1719–20]

Is it possible that again you will do the very same thing I warned you of so lately? I believe you thought I only rallied when I told you the other night I would pester you with letters. Did not I know you very well, I should think you knew but little of the world, to imagine that a woman would not keep her word whenever she promised anything that was malicious. Had not you better a thousand times throw away one hour, at some time or other of the day, then to be interrupted in your business at this rate? For I know 'tis as impossible for you to burn my letters without reading them, as tis for me to avoid reproving you when you behave yourself so wrong. Once more I advise you, if you have any regard for your quiet, to alter your behaviour quickly, for I do assure you I have too much spirit to sit down contented with this treatment. Now, because I love frankness extremely, I here tell you that I have determined to try all manner of human arts to reclaim you, and if all those fail I am resolved to have recourse to the black one, which, [it] is said, never does. Now see what inconveniences you will bring both me and yourself into. Pray think calmly of it. Is it not much better to come of yourself then to be brought by force, and that, perhaps, at a time when you have the most agreeable engagement in the world? For when I undertake anything, I don't love to do it by halves. But there is one thing falls out very luckily for you, which is, that of all the passions revenge hurries me least, so that you have it yet in your power to turn all this fury into good humour, and depend upon it, and more, I assure you. Come at what time you please, you can never fail of being very well received.

JONATHAN SWIFT to VANESSA (ESTHER VANHOMRIGH)

[c. 1720]

If you write as you do, I shall come the seldomer, on purpose to be pleased with your letters, which I never look into without wondering how a Brat, who cannot read, can possibly write so well. . . .

MADELEINE SMITH to PIERRE EMILE L'ANGELIER

[c. 1857]
Tuesday evening, twelve o'clock.

Emile,

I have this night received your note. Oh, it is kind of you to write me. Emile, no one can know the intense agony of mind I have suffered last night and today. Emile, my father's wrath would kill me – you little know his temper. Emile, for the love you once had for me, do not denounce me to my P. Emile, if he should read my letters to you he will put me from him – he will hate me as a guilty wretch. I loved you, and wrote to you in my first ardent love – it was with my deepest love I loved you. It was for your love I adored you. I put on paper what I should not. I was free because I loved you with my heart. If he or any other one saw those fond letters to you, what would not be said of me? On my bended knees I write you, and ask you as you hope for mercy at the judgment day, do not inform on me – do not make me a public shame. Emile, my love has been one of bitter disappointment. You, and only you, can make the rest of my life peaceful. My own conscience will be a punishment that I shall carry to my grave. I have deceived the best of men. You may forgive me, but God never will. For God's love, forgive me, and betray me not. For the love you once had to me, do not bring down my father's wrath on me. It will kill my mother (who is not well). It will forever cause me bitter unhappiness. I am humble before you, and crave your mercy. You can give me forgiveness, and you, oh, you only, can make me happy for the rest of my life. I would not ask you to love me or ever make me your wife. I am too guilty for that. I have deceived and told you too many falsehoods for you ever to respect me. But, oh! will you not keep my secret from the world? Oh! will you not, for Christ's sake, denounce me. I shall be undone. I shall be ruined. Who would trust me? Shame will be my lot. Despise me, hate me, but make me not the public scandal. Forget me for ever. Blot out all remembrance of me . . . I have . . . you ill. I did love you, and it was my soul's ambition to be your wife. I asked you to tell me my faults. You did so, and it made me cool towards you gradually. When you have found fault with me I have cooled. It was not love for another, for there is no one I love. My love has all been given to you. My heart is empty, cold; I am unloved, I am despised. I told you I had ceased to love you – it was true. I did not love as I did; but, oh! till within the time of our coming to town I loved you fondly. I longed to be your wife. I had fixed February. I longed for it. The time I could not leave my father's house, I grew discontented; then I ceased to love you. Oh, Emile, this is indeed the true statement. Now you can know my state of mind. Emile, I have suffered much for you. I lost much of my father's confidence since that September; and my mother has never been the same to me. No, she has never given me the same kind look. For the sake of my mother, her who gave me life, spare me from shame. Oh Emile, will you, in God's name, hear my prayer? I ask God to forgive me. I have prayed that he might put it in your heart to spare me from shame. Never, never, while I live can I be happy. No, no, I shall always have the thought I deceived you. I am guilty; it will be a punishment I shall bear till the day of my death. I am humbled thus to crave your pardon. But I dare not. While I have breath I shall ever think of you as my best friend, if you will only keep this between ourselves. I blush to ask you. Yet, Emile, will you not grant me this my last favour? – if you will never reveal what has passed. Oh, for God's sake, for the love of Heaven, hear me. I grow mad. I have been ill, very ill, all day. I have had what has given me a false spirit. I had resort to what I should not have taken, but my brain is on fire. I feel as if death would indeed be sweet. Denounce me not. Emile, Emile, think of our once happy days. Pardon me if you can: pray for me as the most wretched, guilty, miserable creature on the earth. I could stand anything but my father's hot displeasure. Emile, you will not cause my death. If he is to get your letters, I cannot see him any more; and my poor mother, I will never more kiss her. It would be a shame to them all. Emile, will you not spare me this? Hate me, despise me, but do not expose me. I cannot write more. I am too ill to-night.

P.S. I cannot get to the back stair. I never could see the way to it. I will take you within in the door. The area gate will be open. I shall see you from my window at twelve o'clock. I will wait till one o'clock.

BEGINNINGS

Sarah Bernhardt to Victorien Sardou

[c. 1880s]

Wonderful Boy,

Where are you to-night? Your letter came only an hour ago – cruel hour – I had hoped you would spend it with me here.

Heloise to Abelard

[Twelfth century]

To her master, or rather her father, husband, or rather brother; his handmaid, or rather his daughter, wife, or rather sister; to Abelard, Heloise.

Thomas Jefferson to Maria Cosway

Paris 27 July, 1788

Hail, dear friend of mine! for I am never so happy as when business, smoothing her magisterial brow, says 'I give you an hour to converse with your friends.'

Marcel Proust to Madame Straus

[1892]

Thursday, after leaving you

Madame,

I love mysterious women, since you are one . . .

ENDINGS

CHARLES BAUDELAIRE to MADAME SABATIER

[1857]

Farewell, dear lady. I kiss your hands as a sign of my utter devotion.

All the verses contained between page 84 and page 105 are yours alone.

Charles Baudelaire

JOHANN WOLFGANG VON GOETHE to CHARLOTTE BUFF

Frankfurt, 26 August 1774

... and it seemed to me, that your spirit was about me, and about Karlinchen and Lenchen, everyone, and everything I had not seen, and had seen, and finally there was Lotte, and Lotte and Lotte, and Lotte, and Lotte, and without Lotte nothing but Want and Mourning and Death. Adieu, Lotte, not a word more to-day, 26th August.

BERT FIELDER to NELL FIELDER

[*c.* 1915]
P.S.Please don't cry so much when you write next, as it makes
them in an awful mess.

MARCEL PROUST to MADAME STRAUS

[*c.* 1890s]
... you do not deign to countenance the sentiments which give
me the sad rapture of being
                    The most respectful servant
                    of your Sovereign Indifference
                    Marcel Proust

IN BRIEF

JAMES JOYCE to NORA BARNACLE

60 Shelbourne Road
15 June 1904

I may be blind. I looked for a long time at a head of reddish brown hair and decided it was not yours. I went home quite dejected. I would like to make an appointment but it might not suit you. I hope you will be kind enough to make one with me – if you have not forgotten me!

James A Joyce

NAPOLEON BONAPARTE to JOSEPHINE BONAPARTE

Robervella, 26 Nivose, year V [1797]

To Josephine, in Milan

I have defeated the enemy. Kilmaine will be sending you a copy of the account of the battle. I am dead with exhaustion. I beg you to leave with all speed for Verona; I need you, for I can see that I am heading for a serious illness.

I send you a thousand kisses. I am in bed.

Bonaparte

ROBERT SCHUMANN to CLARA WIECK

On the morning of the 1st, 1838.

What a heavenly morning! All the bells are ringing; the sky is so golden and blue and clear – and before me lies your letter. I send you my first kiss, beloved.

MARIE D'AGOULT to FRANZ LISZT

Basle, 2 June 1835

Let me know by return the name of your inn and the number of your room. Do not go out. My mother is here; my brother-in-law has left. By the time that you read this I shall have spoken, up until now I have not dared say anything.

This is a final harsh test, but my love is my faith and I thirst after martyrdom.

Wednesday. Drei Könige [The Three Kings].

FRANZ LISZT to MARIE D'AGOULT

[2 June 1835]

Here I am in answer to your call.

I shall not go out till I see you. My room is at the Hotel de la Cigogne number twenty at the first étage; – go at the right side.

Yours.

Johann Wolfgang von Goethe to Charlotte von Stein

[*c.* 1780]

Through snow and frost a flower gleams. As my love does through ice and the evil weather of life. Perhaps I shall come today. I am well and tranquil and I believe that I love you more than yesterday. But that belief grows with every single day.

Prince de Joinville to Rachel and her reply

[*c.* 1840]

When, after seeing her act one evening, the Prince de Joinville sent Rachel his card with the famous words: 'Where? – When? – How much?' she countered:

'Your place – Tonight – Free'.

Biographical Details

A

PETER ABELARD (1079–1142) *164, 168, 174, 209*
In 1116 Peter Abelard, the greatest philosopher of his time and a priest,
became Heloise's tutor. Falling in love with her, he 'quitted Aristotle
and his dry maxims to practise the precepts of the more ingenious Ovid'
Heloise fought hard against marriage, knowing it would destroy his
career; he would not be deflected. After the marriage her Uncle Fulbert,
in barbaric revenge, had Peter castrated. Heloise retired to a convent,
Peter wandered from monastery to monastery. Their mutual bitterness and unhappiness was soothed over the years by their continued
exchange of correspondence.
  The Letters of Abelard and Heloise (Penguin Classics, 1974)

MARIE D'AGOULT (1806–1877) *see under* FRANZ LISZT

CZARINA ALEXANDRA (1872–1918) *137*
The 'great & beautiful times' were never to come. Three weeks after
this letter Rasputin, the 'dear Friend', was murdered. The following
year the Russian armies mutinied and the Czar abdicated. He and his
family were held prisoner until July 1918; they were then all executed
by revolutionary firing squad.
  Nicholas and Alexandra by Robert Massie (Gollancz, 1968;
  Atheneum, 1967)
  Letters of the Tsaritsa to the Tsar: 1914–1916 (Duckworth, 1923)

PIERRE EMILE L'ANGELIER *see under* MADELEINE SMITH

ANNA *see under* VINCENT

APOLLONIUS *114*
Taus's lover, Apollonius, was the civil governor of a district in Egypt,

and had to contend with the Jewish revolt of A.D. 117. He had a sister-wife who was also devoted to him. Nothing else is known about Taus. For a glimpse of Apollonius' family life and problems, see

> *Daily Life in Roman Egypt* by Jack Lindsay (Muller, 1963; Barnes & Noble, 1964)

FRANÇOIS MARIE AROUET   *see* VOLTAIRE

FAIR MAID OF ASTOLAT   *40*

In order to disguise himself in a jousting match, Sir Launcelot borrowed Sir Bernard of Astolat's shield. His daughter fell in love with the un-known knight. In due course his identity was discovered, and know-ing that he would never love her, she decided to end her life.

> *Le Morte d'Arthur* by Sir Thomas Malory (Penguin, 1969)

B

WALTER BAGEHOT (1826–1877)   *104*

Elizabeth Wilson was the daughter of James Wilson, founder of the *Economist*. Walter Bagehot wooed her in fine Victorian style – staying with the family at Claverton, their country house, sitting with her in the conservatory, finally asking her father for her hand. The couple were married in 1858. A contemporary said, 'This marriage gave Bagehot nineteen years of undisturbed happiness'.

> *Walter Bagehot* by Norman St John Stevas (Eyre & Spottiswoode, 1959; Indiana University Press, 1959)

HONORÉ DE BALZAC (1799–1850)   *69, 116*

Balzac first met the Polish Countess Evelina Hanska in 1833 when she was still married. They agreed to marry after the death of her elderly husband. After long separations, quarrels and reunions they finally married in 1850, by which time both were getting old and unwell. Sadly, Balzac died three months after the marriage.

> *Prometheus: The Life of Balzac* by André Maurois (Bodley Head, 1965; Harper & Row, 1966)

EMILIE BARDACH (1872–1955)   *see under* HENRIK IBSEN

NORA BARNACLE   *see under* JAMES JOYCE

SARAH BARNARD   *see under* MICHAEL FARADAY

MARIE BASHKIRTSEFF (1860–1884) *16*

On a romantic impulse, Marie Bashkirtseff wrote to Guy de Maupassant under a pseudonym to tell him how much she admired him. Intrigued, he replied. She rapidly tired of his world-weary letters, and soon stopped writing. He never discovered her identity.

The Letters of Marie Bashkirtseff, translated by Mary J. Serrano (Cassell, 1891)

CHARLES BAUDELAIRE (1821–1867) *213*

Mme Sabatier was a courtesan, famed for her kindness and generosity. Disappointed in his other love affairs, Baudelaire began writing her anonymous letters. She was to him neither sister, friend nor mistress, but 'guardian Angel, Muse and Madonna'. When later she discovered his identity and fell in love with him, he took fright and quickly disassociated himself.

Baudelaire: A Self-Portrait–Selected Letters, edited and translated by Lois Boe Hyslop and Francis E. Hyslop (Oxford University Press, 1957)
Baudelaire by Enid Starkie (Faber, 1957; New Directions, 1958)

FELICE BAUER *see under* FRANZ KAFKA

JOSEPHINE DE BEAUHARNAIS (1763–1814) *see under* NAPOLEON BONAPARTE

PIETRO BEMBO (1470–1547) *see under* LUCREZIA BORGIA

SARAH BERNHARDT (1844–1923) *209*

Sarah Bernhardt's romantic – but largely platonic – affection for the poet-playwright Victorien Sardou lasted many years. He wrote a number of plays for her. She is reputed to have said, 'Ah. If I were not Sarah I would like to be Sardou'.

ANTOINE BIBESCO *see under* MARCEL PROUST

ANNE BOLEYN (1507–1536) *see under* HENRY VIII

JOSEPHINE BONAPARTE (1763–1814) *see under* NAPOLEON BONAPARTE, *just below*

NAPOLEON BONAPARTE (1769–1821) *79, 191, 217*

Napoleon and Josephine were married in 1795. Two days after the wedding Napoleon set off on his Italian campaign. Josephine was a poor correspondent, indifferent to Napoleon and flirting with someone else. It was only later that she came to love him. It was with mutual sorrow that he had to divorce her in 1809 for the sake of an heir.

Napoleon Bonaparte: An Intimate Biography by Vincent Cronin (Collins, 1971; William Morrow, 1972)

LUCREZIA BORGIA (1480–1519)   *147*
In 1502 Pietro Bembo was poet at the court of the Duke of Ferrara. Lucrezia, the Duke's wife, found him fascinating. For a summer they were lovers, a dangerous and difficult enterprise in the midst of Borgia family treachery and intrigue. After the death of her father the Pope, the love affair came to an end; but when Bembo became Papal Secretary she continued writing to him

The Life and Times of Lucrezia Borgia by Maria Bellonci (Weidenfeld, 1953; Harcourt, Brace, 1954)

FANNY BRAWNE (1800–1865)   *see under* JOHN KEATS

MARGERY BREWS (d. 1495)   *3, 50*
In 1477 Sir John Paston began considering Margery Brews, daughter of Sir Thomas Brews, as a possible wife. She was very determined to marry him, and gave her mother no peace till she began organising the betrothal. After some wrangling over the dowry they were married.

The Paston Letters, edited by John Warrington (Dent, 1924)

MADAME BRILLON   *see under* BENJAMIN FRANKLIN

THE DUKE OF BUCKINGHAM (1592–1628)   *see under* JAMES I

CHARLOTTE BUFF (1753–1828)   *see under* JOHANN WOLFGANG VON GOETHE

ROBERT BURNS (1759–1796)   *10*
Burns met Agnes Maclehose in Edinburgh in 1787, shortly after she had been deserted by her husband. They soon began corresponding as 'Sylvander' and 'Clarinda'. A Calvinist, she begged Burns to maintain their relationship as one of 'warmest, tenderest, friendship'. They continued writing to each other for two years, until after Burns' marriage to Jean Armour.

Clarinda by Raymond Lamont Brown (Martin Black, 1968)
Robert Burns: The Man and the Poet by Robert Fitzhugh (W. H. Allen, 1971; Houghton Mifflin, 1970)

LORD BYRON (1788–1824)   *82, 84*

'That beautiful pale face will be my fate', wrote Lady Caroline Lamb, on meeting Byron. But he tired of her very quickly; by the time he wrote this last, passionate letter, he had already left her. On going to Italy in 1819 he met Teresa Guiccioli. His affair with her had all the elements of Italian opera buffa – an elderly husband, a young wife, elopements, gossiping villagers. They lived together for two years before Byron left to fight in Greece in 1823.

> *Byron: A Self-Portrait, Letters and Diaries,* edited by Peter
> Quennell (John Murray, 1950; Scribner's, 1950)
> *Byron* by Peter Quennell (Collins, 1974; Haskell House, 1974)

C

JANE WELSH CARLYLE (1802–1866)   *21, 67, 133, 134*

The Carlyles were married for forty years, a marriage often tempestuous and difficult. They found their tenderest expression for each other in their letters. Jane staunchly supported Carlyle all her life. When she died in 1866, he was stricken with remorse to discover from her letters and diaries how unhappy her life had been.

> *Jane Welsh Carlyle: A New Selection of Her Letters,* arranged by
> Trudy Bliss (Gollancz, 1949; Macmillan, 1950)
> *The Carlyles: A Biography of Thomas and Jane Carlyle* by John
> Stewart Collis (Sidgwick and Jackson, 1971; Dodd, Mead, 1973)

THOMAS CARLYLE (1795–1881)   *see under* JANE WELSH CARLYLE, *just above*

(DORA) CARRINGTON (1892–1932)   *33, 177, 180*

Mark Gertler's passion for Carrington, whom he met at the Slade School of Fine Art in 1910, was never really reciprocated. They were constantly quarrelling as she failed to meet the intense demands he made on her. In 1915 she met Lytton Strachey, whose gentle detachment and homosexuality were a relief after the storms of her relationship with Gertler. She became deeply attached to Strachey, going to live with him in 1917. When Ralph Patridge fell in love with her, she reluctantly agreed to marry him; for a while the three of them lived together. Eventually this proved an unhappy arrangement and Ralph moved out. In 1932 Strachey died of cancer; Carrington shot herself a month later.

> *Carrington: Letters and Extracts from Her Diaries,* chosen and with

an introduction by David Garnett (Cape, 1970; Holt, Rinehart and Winston, 1971)

CATHERINE OF ARAGON (1485–1536)   *125*
In spite of everything she had endured from Henry VIII – the humiliation of the divorce, exile from the court, separation from her beloved daughter Mary – Catherine remained devoted and loving to the man she considered her rightful husband until her death.
  Catherine of Aragon by Garrett Mattingly (Cape, 1942; Little, Brown, 1941)

CHARLES I (1600–1649)   *115*
During the Civil War Henrietta Maria was forced to flee to France. Charles wrote her many desperate and pathetic letters, but they never met again. She was only told of his execution a month after it took place.
  The Letters of King Charles I, edited by Sir Charles Petrie (Cassell, 1935)
  Charles I by John Bowle (Weidenfeld, 1975)

GERTRUDE CHATAWAY   *see under* CHARLES DODGSON

ANTON CHEKHOV (1860–1904)   *114, 139*
Chekhov met Olga Knipper in 1898. He married her, somewhat against his will, in 1901. As an actress she spent long months in Moscow, whilst Chekhov pined for her in Yalta, where he was confined because of his TB. Though he had always said he wanted a wife 'who, like the moon, will not appear in my sky every day', he found life cold and comfortless during her frequent absences. She was constantly torn between tenderness for him and the excitement of her life in Moscow.
  Anton Chekhov's Life and Thought: Selected Letters and Commentary, translated by Michael Henry Heim and Simon Karlinsky (Bodley Head, 1973; University of California Press, 1975)
  Chekhov by Ernest Simmons (Cape, 1963; Little, Brown, 1964)

FRÉDÉRIC CHOPIN (1810–1849)   *158*
Chopin's affair with Delphine Potocka, beginning late in 1832 and lasting until she left Paris in 1836, antedates his relationship with George Sand. Delphine later became the mistress of Zygmunt Krasinski, the great Polish poet.
  The Life and Death of Chopin by Casimir Wierzynski (Simon and Schuster, 1949)

CLARINDA (1759–1841)   *see under* ROBERT BURNS

MARIA COSWAY (1759–1838)   *see under* THOMAS JEFFERSON

JEAN COUCHAUD   *see under* ROBERT DE MONTESQUIOU

ELIZABETH CROMWELL   *see under* OLIVER CROMWELL, *just below*

OLIVER CROMWELL (1599–1658)   *135, 136*
Cromwell married Elizabeth Bourchier, the daughter of a wealthy
London merchant, when he was 21 and she 23. There was always a
bond of very deep affection between them.
   Cromwell: The Lord Protector by Antonia Fraser (Weidenfeld,
   1973; Knopf, 1973)

MADAME CURIAL   *see under* STENDHAL

PIERRE CURIE (1859–1906)   *8*
Pierre Curie met Marie Sklodovska when he was 35. She was the first
woman to intrigue him on a level both intellectual and romantic, the
first woman able to appreciate and understand his scientific research.
She refused him at first, but gradually was drawn to him. They married in 1895.
   Marie Curie by Robert Reid (Collins, 1974; Saturday Review Press,
   1974)

D

CAMILLE DESMOULINS (1760–1794)   *122*
Camille Desmoulins, revolutionary and one-time friend of Robes-
pierre's, was executed four days after writing this letter, in spite of
the efforts of his beloved wife, Lucile, to save him. She was guillotined
two weeks later.
   Camille Desmoulins by J. B. Morton (Werner Laurie, 1951)

LUCILE DESMOULINS (1771–1794)   *see under* CAMILLE DESMOULINS, *just
   above*

DENIS DIDEROT (1713–1784)   *195*
Sophie Volland was in her 40s when the philosopher and encyclopedist
Diderot met and began courting her. Jealous, her mother took her away
for long months to the country. Diderot never lived with his mistress,
but they continued corresponding all their lives.

[227]

Diderot's Letters to Sophie Volland, a selection translated by Peter France (Oxford University Press, 1972)

Diderot by Arthur M. Wilson (Oxford University Press, 1972)

BENJAMIN DISRAELI (1804–1881) *4*

Disraeli, the future Prime Minister, *had* touched Mary Anne Wyndham Lewis' heart. They were married in August 1839, and were extremely happy together.

Disraeli by Robert Blake (Eyre & Spottiswoode, 1966; St. Martin's Press, 1966)

CHARLES DODGSON (LEWIS CARROLL) (1832–1898) *99*

Gertrude Chataway was one of the many little girls to whom Lewis Carroll addressed his charming, funny letters. She was a favourite, one of the few children he continued to see when grown up.

Victoria Through the Looking Glass by Florence Becker Lennon (Simon and Schuster, 1945; *The Life of Lewis Carroll,* 3rd ed., Dover, 1972)

DORELIA (DOROTHY MC NEILL) *see under* IDA JOHN

LORD ALFRED DOUGLAS (1870–1945) *see under* OSCAR WILDE

JULIETTE DROUET (1806–1883) *see under* VICTOR HUGO

OLYMPE DUNOYER *see under* VOLTAIRE

F

MICHAEL FARADAY (1791–1867) *50*

In spite of the English physicist and chemist Faraday's protestations of being a bad letter writer, Sarah Barnard accepted him. They were very happily married.

Michael Faraday by L. Pearce Williams (Chapman & Hall, 1965; Basic Books, 1965)

BERT FIELDER (1882–1916) *112, 214*

Bert Fielder never lived to 'carry on the old life once more'. He was killed in October 1916. There is no record of what happened to Nell or the Boy.

A Place Called Armageddon: Letters from the Great War, edited by Michael Moynihan (David & Charles, 1975)

NELL FIELDER   *see under* BERT FIELDER, *just above*

F. SCOTT FITZGERALD (1896–1940)   *see under* ZELDA FITZGERALD, *just below*

ZELDA FITZGERALD (1900–1948)   *48, 92, 182*
Zelda Sayre and F. Scott Fitzgerald were married in 1920. With their golden looks, talent and glamour they came to epitomise the atmosphere of the Jazz Age. By 1929 the marriage was cracking up: Zelda had the first of her many breakdowns; Scott was drinking more and more heavily. He died in 1940 of a heart attack, she in 1948 in a hospital fire.
   Zelda Fitzgerald by Nancy Milford (Bodley Head, 1970; Harper
   & Row, 1970)

ADÈLE FOUCHER   *see under* VICTOR HUGO

BENJAMIN FRANKLIN (1706–1790)   *94*
Franklin was 70, Mme Brillon in her 30s when they met in Paris. Their elaborate and flirtatious courtship on paper developed, to Franklin's slight disappointment, into nothing more than an *amitié amoureuse*, with Mme Brillon addressing him as 'mon cher Papa'. They continued corresponding for years after Franklin's return to America.
   Mr Franklin: A Selection from His Personal Letters, edited by
   Leonard W. Labarée and Whitfield Bell, Jr (Oxford University
   Press, 1956; Yale University Press, 1956)
   Mon Cher Papa: Franklin and the Ladies of Paris by Claude-Anne
   Lopez (Yale University Press, 1966)

JILL FURSE (1915–1945)   *142*
Jill Furse was a beautiful and talented young actress when the poet Laurence Whistler met her in the 1930s. Married in 1939, they were separated for most of the war, but achieved a remarkable closeness that amounted often to telepathy. She died tragically in 1945, after giving birth to their second child.
   The Initials in the Heart by Laurence Whistler (Hart-Davis, 1964)

G

MARK GERTLER   *see under* (DORA) CARRINGTON

JOHANN WOLFGANG VON GOETHE (1749–1832)   *213, 219*
Charlotte Buff was Goethe's first love. She was engaged when he met

her; he was happy to love unhappily, seeking the image, not the reality, of love. Baroness Charlotte von Stein, though married, was loved by Goethe for ten years. She educated him in the ways and manners of the Weimar court, but he left her for a cheerful, uneducated peasant girl. Charlotte von Stein declined into a bitter and lonely old age.

> *Letters from Goethe,* translated by M. von Herzfeld and C. Melvil Sym (Edinburgh University Press, 1957)
> *Goethe: His Life and Times* by Richard Friedenthal (Weidenfeld, 1965; World, 1965)

EFFIE GRAY (1828–1897)   *see under* JOHN RUSKIN

HIPPOLYTE DE GUIBERT (1743–1790)   *see under* JULIE DE LESPINASSE

TERESA GUICCIOLI (1801–1873)   *see under* LORD BYRON

H

ALEXANDER HAMILTON (1755–1804)   *110*

Alexander Hamilton married Elizabeth Schuyler in 1780. Nearly twenty years later he declared that 'It is impossible to be happier than I am in a wife'.

> *Alexander Hamilton* by Broadus Mitchell (Crowell, 1970)

MRS HAMILTON   *see under* ALEXANDER HAMILTON, *just above*

COUNTESS HANSKA   *see under* HONORÉ DE BALZAC

FRANK HARRIS (1854–1931)   *190*

In the mid-twenties Harris dictated volumes of his autobiography to a series of secretaries, most of whom were in love with him, all of whom he hoped to titillate. He himself was impotent by then. 'Rita' (Erika Lorenz) he met in Berlin, and quickly persuaded to come and work for him. After a few months the affair ended sourly; she was unceremoniously bundled back to Germany by Harris's wife; he accused her of the theft of some of his manuscript.

> *Frank Harris* by Philippa Pullar (Hamish Hamilton, 1975; Simon and Schuster, 1976)

NATHANIEL HAWTHORNE (1804–1864)   *71, 72*

For a long while after leaving Bowdoin College, Hawthorne lived a solitary life. Then in 1838 he met Sophia Amelia Peabody, and in 1842 married her. They were deeply happy. 'My wife is, in the strictest sense, my sole companion, and I need no other. There is no vacancy in my mind any more than in my heart', he wrote.

> *Nathaniel Hawthorne and His Wife: A Biography* by Julian
> Hawthorne (Archon, 1968, reprint of 1884 edition)

LAURE HAYMAN   *see under* MARCEL PROUST

HELOISE (1097–1164)   *see under* PETER ABELARD

HENRIETTA MARIA (1609–1669)   *see under* CHARLES I

HENRY VIII (1491–1547)   *17, 111*

For six years Henry was obsessed with love for Anne Boleyn. Prudently avoiding becoming his mistress, she became his wife in 1533 after he caused his marriage to Catherine of Aragon to be annulled. By the following year he was flirting seriously with Jane Seymour. Accusing Anne (probably falsely) of incest, treason and adultery, he had her tried and executed in 1536. Almost immediately he married Jane.

> *Henry VIII* by J. J. Scarisbrick (Eyre & Spottiswoode, 1968;
> University of California Press, 1968)
> *The Love Letters of Henry VIII*, edited by Henry Savage (Allan
> Wingate, 1949)

ELIZABETH HERVEY   *see under* JOHN HERVEY, FIRST EARL OF BRISTOL,
 just below

JOHN HERVEY, FIRST EARL OF BRISTOL (1665–1751)   *143, 144*

Elizabeth Hervey was John Hervey's second wife. He was a plain country gentleman, while she was a courtier, a lady of the bedchamber to Queen Caroline; he was all for exercise and fresh air, she for drugs, potions and apothecaries. In spite of their differences in temperament, their life together was harmonious and contented. He wrote as tender letters to her after thirty years of marriage as at the beginning of their life together.

> *The Letter-Books of John Hervey*, edited by S. H. A. Hervey
> (Ernest Jackson, 1894)

COUNTESS SOPHIE D'HOUDETOT (1730–1813)   *see under* JEAN JACQUES
 ROUSSEAU

VICTOR HUGO (1802–1884)   *61, 81, 149*
Victor Hugo fell in love with Adèle Foucher when she was 16 and he 17. Secretly engaged for three years – his parents strenuously opposed the match – they were eventually married in 1822. Adèle rapidly became disenchanted with her husband's infidelities; the most serious of these was his affair with Juliette Drouet, an actress. Hugo's love affair with her was life-long. She gave up the stage to please him, and lived a largely secluded life.

> *Juliette Drouet's Love Letters to Victor Hugo,* edited by Louis Cuimbaud, translated by Lady Theodora Davidson (Stanley Paul & Co, 1915)
>
> *Olimpio: The Life of Victor Hugo* by André Maurois (Cape, 1956; Harper & Row, 1956)

AGLAÉ DE HUNOLSTEIN   *36*
Aglaé de Hunolstein was one of the court circle of Marie Antoinette. She was indifferent to the Marquis's wooing until he returned, glorious, from fighting the British in America. Malicious gossip destroyed much of their happiness, and this, together with her family's anger at the affair, compelled her to end it. She left the court and went into a convent.

> *Lady in Waiting: The Romance of Lafayette and Aglaé de Hunolstein* by Louis R. Gottschalk (Johns Hopkins University Press, 1939)

I

HENRIK IBSEN (1828–1906)   *53*
Emilie Bardach was 18, Ibsen 61 when they met. Though the encounter provoked strong emotions in both of them, the affair never flowered beyond the correspondence. As a source of inspiration for his work, though, she was of great importance.

> *Letters and Speeches,* edited by E. Springhorn (MacGibbon & Kee, 1965; Hill & Wang, 1965)
>
> *Ibsen* by Michael Meyer (Hart-Davis, 1967)

GILBERT IMLAY   *see under* MARY WOLLSTONECRAFT

ISISDORA   *see under* SERENOS

J

JAMES I (1566–1625) *82*

George Villiers, the Duke of Buckingham, was James I's last favourite; he spoiled and doted on him into his maudlin old age. Permissive toward all the king's foibles, Buckingham became almost more powerful than the king, a focal point of discontent in the country.

King James VI and I by D. H. Wilson (Cape, 1956)

THOMAS JEFFERSON (1743–1826) *103, 209*

Jefferson's wife died in 1782. Despatched to France as Minister following Franklin, he met Maria Cosway, young and very unhappily married. Their love affair was intense but intermittent as she frequently had to leave Paris with her husband. Eventually she fled to Italy with a castrato singer, and later founded a convent school for girls. Jefferson returned to America.

The Family Letters of Thomas Jefferson, edited by Edwin M. Betts and James A. Bear (University of Missouri Press, 1966)
Thomas Jefferson: An Intimate History by Fawn M. Brodie (Norton, 1974)

LEO JOGICHES *see under* ROSA LUXEMBURG

IDA JOHN (1873–1906) *87*

The painter Augustus John married Ida Nettleship in 1901. John loved mysteriousness in women; on marriage this quality inevitably disappeared. Two years later he fell in love with Dorelia (Dorothy McNeill). Though initially jealous of Dorelia, Ida came to like her and for some time the three formed a ménage à trois. Ida was at her happiest living with her children and with Dorelia in Paris. Ida died in 1906 of puerperal fever.

Augustus John by Michael Holroyd (Heinemann, 1974; Holt, Rinehart and Winston, 1975)

PRINCE DE JOINVILLE (1818–1900) *219*

The third son of Louis Philippe, the Prince led an adventurous life as world traveller and sailor. In Paris briefly during the 1840s he had an affair with Rachel (Élisa Félix), one of the most celebrated actresses of the day. Later he married the sister of the Emperor of Brazil. Rachel developed a taste for royal lovers, later including Prince Napoleon on her list.

JAMES JOYCE (1882–1941) *21, 45, 217*

In the summer of 1904 James Joyce met a red-haired girl from Galway named Nora Barnacle. Told of Nora's surname, Joyce's father remarked, 'She'll never leave him', a remark that turned out to be true. They started living together in 1905 and were eventually married.

The Letters of James Joyce, edited by Richard Ellman (Faber, 1966; Viking, 1966)

James Joyce by Richard Ellman (Oxford University Press, 1959)

JUDY *13*

In Rosamond Lehmann's novel, Roddy's brutal rejection shatters the romantic world of Judith's youth. She pines; briefly considers marriage to another man; and slowly begins to break the spell.

Dusty Answer by Rosamond Lehmann (Chatto & Windus, 1927; Henry Holt, 1927)

K

FRANZ KAFKA (1883–1924) *187, 188, 189*

Kafka began writing the first of many thousands of letters to Felice in 1912, shortly after he met her. Twice he became engaged to her; twice he broke it off. His agonising indecision over whether to marry caused her much unhappiness. By 1917 he knew that he had TB and decided to end the affair.

Letters to Felice, edited by Erich Heller and Juergen Born, translated by James Stern and Elisabeth Duckworth (Secker & Warburg, 1974; Schocken, 1973)

Franz Kafka: A Biography by Max Brod (Secker & Warburg, 1947; Schocken, 1947)

JOHN KEATS (1795–1821) *77, 94, 155*

Shortly after Keats met Fanny Brawne in 1818 he became aware that he had TB and would never be able to marry. His love for Fanny was intense, obsessive, jealous and unfulfilled. In 1821 he left for Rome, where he died.

The Letters of John Keats, edited by Maurice Buxton Forman (Oxford University Press, 1935)

John Keats by Robert Gittings (Heinemann, 1968; Little, Brown, 1968)

OLGA KNIPPER (1870?–1959) *see under* ANTON CHEKHOV

L

MARQUIS DE LAFAYETTE (1757–1834)   *see under* AGLAÉ DE HUNOLSTEIN

LADY CAROLINE LAMB (1785–1828)   *see under* LORD BYRON

SIR LAUNCELOT   *see under* FAIR MAID OF ASTOLAT

NINON DE LENCLOS (*c.* 1620–1705)   *34*
Ninon de Lenclos was the wittiest and most beautiful of French courtesans, famed as a 'Venus for her beauty and a Minerva for her wit'! Her affair with the Marquis Henri de Sévigné lasted a bare three months. Banished from her, he immediately consoled himself with Mme Goudron: challenged to a duel because of her, he accepted and was killed.
   Mademoiselle Libertine by Edgar Cohen (Cassell, 1971; Houghton
   Mifflin, 1971)

JULIE DE LESPINASSE (1732–1776)   *78*
Julie de Lespinasse loved writer and soldier Comte Hippolyte de Guibert 'to excess, to distraction, with rapture, with despair'. He was almost totally indifferent to her. When he married in 1776, she wasted away and died, knowing that he had never even been worthy of her love.
   Mlle de Lespinasse: Love Letters to and from the Comte de Guibert,
   translated by E. H. F. Mills (Routledge, 1929)
   A Muse in Love by Margaret Mitchiner (Bodley Head, 1962)

SINCLAIR LEWIS (1885–1951)   *see under* DOROTHY THOMPSON

FRANZ LISZT (1811–1886)   *66, 218*
When Liszt met Marie d'Agoult in 1833 she was married with two children. In 1835 they eloped. Secluded, they were very happy, but Liszt craved success and adulation too much to remain with Marie. His frequent absences on concert tours and his love of fame eventually tired her. The liaison, which had produced three daughters, broke up in 1844.
   The Man Liszt by Ernest Newman (Gollancz, 1969; Taplinger, 1970)

ROSA LUXEMBURG (1870–1919)   *23*
In 1900 Leo Jogiches joined Rosa Luxemburg in Berlin. But neither had the temperament for stable domestic bliss; both were committed to their international political work. In retaliation at a love affair of

his, she took a new lover in 1907; enraged, he threatened to kill both of them. Only much later did their relationship again become friendly. Both died in 1919 during the Spartakist uprising in Germany; Rosa was murdered, Leo executed.

Rosa Luxemburg by J. P. Nettl (Oxford University Press, 1966)

M

AGNES MACLEHOSE (1759–1841)   *see under* ROBERT BURNS

QUEEN MARY II (1662–1694)   *51*
At 15 Mary Stuart was married to William of Orange, twelve years older than she, 'a professional soldier and a plain man'. After a rebellious period, she came to love him deeply; his self-imposed loneliness and inarticulacy prevented him ever expressing his love to the same degree.

Mary II: Queen of England by Hester Chapman (Cape, 1953)

GUY DE MAUPASSANT (1850–1893)   *see under* MARIE BASHKIRTSEFF

NADEJDA VON MECK (1831–1894)   *90*
For thirteen years Mme von Meck was Tchaikovsky's benefactress, though they never met. She supported him, consoled him and wrote to him almost daily. When she abruptly discontinued the correspondence, he became bitter and sad.

Beloved Friend by Catherine Drinker Bowen and Barbara von Meck (Hutchinson, 1937; Random House, 1937)

COUNT GABRIEL HONORÉ DE MIRABEAU (1749–1791)   *47*
At his father's request, Mirabeau was imprisoned in the Château d'If for wasting his own and his wife's fortunes. There he met Sophie de Monnier, the young wife of an elderly magistrate. They eloped, but after three happy months Mirabeau was recaptured. When he came out of prison four years later their feeling for each other had quietly died.

Mirabeau by Oliver J. G. Welch (Cape, 1951)

SOPHIE DE MONNIER   *see under* COUNT GABRIEL HONORÉ DE MIRABEAU, *just above*

ROBERT DE MONTESQUIOU (1855–1921)   *39*
In his old age, Robert de Montesquiou, aesthete, poet and critic, noticed a photo of a beautiful young man on the piano at the home of

his friends the Couchauds. For a year he corresponded with this young man, Jean Couchaud; their meeting proved a great disappointment, and the letters soon ceased.

Prince of Aesthetes: Count Robert de Montesquiou by Philippe Jullian, translated by John Haylock and Francis King (Secker & Warburg, 1967; Viking, 1968)

SIR THOMAS MORE (1478–1535) *121*
For his refusal to take the oath repudiating papal supremacy, Sir Thomas More was executed the day after writing this letter. Margaret Roper, his daughter, was a woman of tremendous courage; with her father dead and her husband in the Tower, she did not mope, but set about teaching his children the difficult scholastic subjects her father had once so lovingly taught her.

Saint Thomas More: Selected Letters, edited by Elizabeth Frances Rogers (Yale University Press, 1961)
Thomas More by R. W. Chambers (Cape, 1935; Harcourt, Brace 1935)

LOUISA DE MORNAND *see under* MARCEL PROUST

WOLFGANG AMADEUS MOZART (1756–1791) *89*
In 1781 Mozart was living in Vienna at the Webers' house. Writing to assure his father of his indifference to Constanze, his landlady's daughter, he soon fell in love with her. In spite of her coquetry, he married her in 1782. His father's grudging consent arrived the day after the marriage.

The Letters of Mozart to His Family, edited by Emily Anderson (Macmillan, 1966; St. Martin's Press, 1966)
The Life and Death of Mozart by Michael Levey (Weidenfeld, 1972; Stein & Day, 1972)

ALFRED DE MUSSET (1810–1857) *9*
George Sand (pseudonym of Amandine Aurore Dupin), novelist, journalist, feminist, was 29 when de Musset, a poet, met her; he was 23. Their relationship developed throughout a series of brutal rejections and ecstatic reunions; their mutual passion was rarely joyous; their unhappiness finally made them part. He remained in love with her all his life.

Alfred: The Passionate Life of Alfred de Musset by Charlotte Haldane (Anthony Blond, 1960)

[237]

N

CZAR NICHOLAS II (1868–1918)   *see under* CZARINA ALEXANDRA

O

DOROTHY OSBORNE (1627–1695)   *55, 154, 193*
William Temple, statesman, diplomat and essayist, and Dorothy Osborne were both Royalists. Separated by William's father, who considered the match unsuitable, they continued their courtship for seven years. They were married in 1654, a 'marriage of souls' as he called it.

> *The Letters of Dorothy Osborne,* edited by G. C. Moore Smith
> (Oxford University Press, 1928)
> *Two Quiet Lives* by Lord David Cecil (Constable, 1948;
> Bobbs-Merrill, 1948)

KATHARINE O'SHEA   *see under* CHARLES STEWART PARNELL, *just below*

P

CHARLES STEWART PARNELL (1846–1891)   *111*
In 1880 Parnell, the fiery champion of Irish Home Rule, fell in love with Katharine O'Shea, the estranged wife of a parliamentary colleague. For many years they lived together secretly as man and wife. When O'Shea divorced his wife in 1890 on the grounds of her adultery, Parnell did not defend himself. The scandal ruined Parnell's political life. He died the following year.

> *The Uncrowned Queen of Ireland: The Life of 'Kitty' O'Shea* by
> Joyce Marlow (Weidenfeld, 1975; Saturday Review Press, 1975)

SIR JOHN PASTON (1442–1479)   *see under* MARGERY BREWS

SOPHIA AMELIA PEABODY (1811–1871)   *see under* NATHANIEL HAWTHORNE

SIR JOHN PELHAM   *see under* LADY PELHAM, *just below*

LADY PELHAM   *109*
This is the earliest known love letter in the English language. Whilst her husband was away with Henry of Lancaster at Ravenspur, Lady Pelham was forced to withstand the siege of Pevensey Castle by Richard II's partisans. Pelham was knighted at Henry IV's coronation in October 1399.

DELPHINE POTOCKA   *see under* FREDERIC CHOPIN

MARCEL PROUST (1871–1922)   *100, 101, 148, 210, 214*
Proust met Antoine Bibesco in 1900; he was one of a group of hetero-
sexual men with whom Proust had long and close friendships. Bibesco
became his friend and correspondent for life, as did Louisa de Mornand.
Proust had a brief affair with her, whilst she was quarrelling with her
lover. Laure Hayman and Mme Straus were both salonnières, older
women whom Proust admired and who were his loyal friends for
many years.
   Letters of Marcel Proust, translated and edited by Mina Curtiss
   (Chatto, 1950; Random House, 1949)
   Marcel Proust by George Painter (Chatto, 1961; Little, Brown, 1959)

GOPAL PURI   *153*
Professor Puri continued to encourage his wife in her education and
she is now a writer and an expert in yoga and cookery. Their relationship developed beyond his dominance after the birth of their children
and they remain very happily married, living and working near
Liverpool.

KAILASH PURI   *see under* GOPAL PURI, *just above*

R

RACHEL (1820–1858)   *see under* PRINCE DE JOINVILLE

ELIZABETH RALEGH   *see under* SIR WALTER RALEGH, *just below*

SIR WALTER RALEGH (1552–1618)   *127*
Ralegh – explorer, courtier, poet and historian – was not, in fact, executed immediately. Confined to the Tower with his wife and son from
1603 until 1616, he was then released by James I to search the Orinoco
for gold. Failure led to his execution at Whitehall in 1618.
   Sir Walter Ralegh: Selections from His Writings and Letters, edited
   by Grace E. Hadow (Clarendon Press, 1917)
   That Great Lucifer by Margaret Irwin (Chatto, 1960; Harcourt,
   Brace, 1960)

RITA (ERIKA LORENZ)   *see under* FRANK HARRIS

RODDY   *see under* JUDY

MARGARET ROPER   *see under* SIR THOMAS MORE

JEAN JACQUES ROUSSEAU (1712–1778)   *38*

Rousseau was 45 when he met the Countess d'Houdetot, mistress of his friend the Marquis de Saint-Lambert. For a brief three months he was inflamed with love for her. Then she panicked about discovery and the affair turned into a sordid story of deceit, guilt and embarrassment, with Rousseau desperately covering his tracks. Rousseau later said that she was 'the first and only love of my life'.

> *Citizen of Geneva: Selections from the Letters of Jean Jacques Rousseau*, edited by Charles Hendel (Oxford University Press, 1937)

BENJAMIN RUSH (1745?–1813)   *141*

Benjamin Rush, American physician, humanitarian and politician – and signer of the Declaration of Independence – married Julia Stockton in 1776. She was a devout, self-effacing woman, who seems to have accepted her husband's view that with marriage 'subordination of your sex to ours is enforced by nature, by reason and by revelation'.

> *The Letters of Benjamin Rush*, edited by Lyman Henry Butterfield (Oxford University Press, 1952; Princeton University Press, 1951)
> *Benjamin Rush: Revolutionary Gadfly* by David Harke (Bobbs-Merrill, 1973)

JULIA RUSH   *see under* BENJAMIN RUSH, *just above*

JOHN RUSKIN (1819–1900)   *92, 93*

In 1848 John Ruskin married Effie Gray. Six years later she wrote bitterly to her parents that she had 'never been told the duties of married persons to each other and knew little or nothing about their relations in the closest union on earth. John avowed no intention of making me his wife'. She left him, their marriage was annulled and she married the painter John Millais.

> *The Ruskins and the Grays* by Mary Lutyens (John Murray, 1972)
> *John Ruskin* by Joan Evans (Cape, 1954; Oxford University Press, 1954)

S

MADAME SABATIER   *see under* CHARLES BAUDELAIRE

GEORGE SAND (1804–1876)   *see under* ALFRED DE MUSSET

VICTORIEN SARDOU (1831–1908)   *see under* SARAH BERNHARDT

ROBERT SCHUMANN (1810–1856)   *64, 218*
Schumann fell in love with Clara Wieck, the daughter of his piano teacher. Herr Wieck bitterly opposed the match, thinking Schumann too poor and too foolhardy for his brilliantly talented daughter. Eventually they applied to a Court of Appeal and were granted permission to marry. They married in 1840 and for a long time were exceptionally happy until Schumann began to show the first signs of schizophrenia; committed to an asylum in 1854, he died two years later.
   The Letters of Robert Schumann, edited by Dr Karl Storck (John Murray, 1907)
   Schumann by Joan Chissell (Dent, 1967; Farrar, Straus & Giroux, 1967)

ELIZABETH SCHUYLER   *see under* ALEXANDER HAMILTON

MARY SCURLOCK   *see under* SIR RICHARD STEELE

SERENOS   *193*
There is no record of what it was that distressed Serenos, nor whether Isisdora came to see him. For more information about marriages of the second century A.D., see
   Daily Life in Roman Egypt by Jack Lindsay (Muller, 1963; Barnes & Noble, 1964)

THE MARQUIS DE SÉVIGNÉ (d. 1651)   *see under* NINON DE LENCLOS

GEORGE BERNARD SHAW (1856–1950)   *see under* ELLEN TERRY

LADY SHIGENARI   *163*
Lady Shigenari, true to her word, took her own life and shortly afterwards her husband was killed in battle. His death made him a perfect exemplar of the Japanese ideal of a 'noble failure' and he became one of his nation's much loved heroes.

LORD KIMURA SHIGENARI   *see under* LADY SHIGENARI, *just above*

MARIE SKLODOVSKA (1867–1934)   *see under* PIERRE CURIE

MADELEINE SMITH (1836–1928)   *203*
In 1855 Madeleine Smith, who came from a wealthy middle-class Glasgow family, became infatuated with a young clerk, Pierre Emile l'Angelier. He was poor, and thus ineligible; her father disapproved.

She continued writing to him, and by 1856 became his mistress, letting him into the house by the back stairs when everyone else was asleep. She soon tired of him when a more eligible suitor appeared. Pierre refused to return her letters and threatened to blackmail her. In March 1857 he died of arsenic poisoning. In a sensational case she was tried for murder, but acquitted on a verdict of 'Not Proven'. She died in the United States in poverty and oblivion at 92.

The Trial of Madeleine Smith, edited by F. Tennyson Jesse (William Hodge, 1927)

RICHARD STEELE (1672–1729) *158*
Soon after the death of his first wife, Richard Steele began courting Mary Scurlock. They were married in 1707. 'The business of my life', he later wrote, 'is to make you easy and happy'. For her part she found him 'as agreeable and pleasant a man as any in England'.

The Correspondence of Richard Steele, edited by Rae Blanchard (Oxford University Press, 1941)
Sir Richard Steele by Willard Connely (Cape, 1934; Scribner's, 1934)

CHARLOTTE VON STEIN (1742–1827) *see under* JOHANN WOLFGANG VON GOETHE

STENDHAL (1783–1842) *22, 194*
Mme Clementine Amelie Curial was one of the great loves of the writer Stendhal's life. She was married to a man fourteen years her senior, a brutal and unfaithful man. Her passion for Stendhal (pseudonym of Marie Henri Beyle) led them into reckless behaviour; she hid him in her cellar for days on end. But she found the affair tormenting, and tried to commit suicide. She broke with him in 1826.

Stendhal by Joanna Richardson (Gollancz, 1974; Coward, McCann & Geoghegan, 1974)

LYTTON STRACHEY (1880–1932) *see under* (DORA) CARRINGTON

MADAME STRAUS *see under* MARCEL PROUST

JONATHAN SWIFT (1667–1745) *24, 25, 26, 202, 203*
Swift felt for Vanessa (Esther Vanhomrigh) 'an entire affection' that fell short of the admiration and love she felt for him. Discovering his relationship with Stella (Esther Johnson), whom he had long loved, she

became jealous. Her possessiveness made Swift leave her. Overcome with misery, Vanessa died soon after.

Vanessa and Her Correspondence with Jonathan Swift, edited and introduced by A. Martin Freeman (Selwyn & Blount, 1921)

Jonathan Swift by Nigel Dennis (Macmillan, 1965)

T

TAUS   *see under* APOLLONIUS

PIOTR TCHAIKOVSKY (1840–1893)   *see under* NADEJDA VON MECK

WILLIAM TEMPLE (1628–1699)   *see under* DOROTHY OSBORNE

ELLEN TERRY (1847–1928)   *91*
In 1892 George Bernard Shaw began his correspondence with Ellen Terry. Both adored their paper courtship, both feared that a meeting might spoil it. It did. They met in 1900, and thereafter the correspondence dwindled away.

Ellen Terry and Bernard Shaw: A Correspondence, edited by Christopher St John (Constable, 1931; Putnam's, 1931)

Ellen Terry by Roger Manvell (Heinemann, 1968; Putnam's, 1968)

THEON (AND THEON HIS FATHER)   *27*
There is no known reply to this letter. For other references to 'little Theon' and commentary on children of the time, see

Daily Life in Roman Egypt by Jack Lindsay (Muller, 1963; Barnes & Noble, 1964)

DOROTHY THOMPSON (1894–1961)   *183*
Dorothy Thompson, the distinguished American journalist, met Sinclair Lewis at a dinner party she gave in 1927. He proposed the first evening they met, and kept on proposing until she accepted him. The marriage very soon turned out to be a failure. He was jealous of her work, she became bored with his way of life. In 1937 they separated, in 1942 they were divorced.

Dorothy and Red by Vincent Sheean (Heinemann, 1964; Houghton Mifflin, 1963)

AGNES TICHBORNE   *see under* CHIDIOCK TICHBORNE, *just below*

CHIDIOCK TICHBORNE (1558–1586)   *126*
Chidiock Tichborne was executed the day after writing this letter for

his part in the Babington plot, which was designed to overthrow Elizabeth I and put Mary Stuart on the throne.

Mary Queen of Scots by Antonia Fraser (Weidenfeld, 1969; Delacorte, 1969)

V

VANESSA (ESTHER VANHOMRIGH) (1690–1723) *see under* JONATHAN SWIFT

VINCENT *31*

In Jean Rhys's novel, Anna drifts from her exhausting life as a chorus girl into a quiet, happy liaison with Walter. After Vincent's curt letter she loses all sense of purpose in her life. She begins to flit aimlessly from lover to lover, joyless, ill, unloved and unloving, dreaming only of the beauties of her youth in the West Indies.

Voyage in the Dark by Jean Rhys (Constable, 1934; Morrow, 1934)

SOPHIE VOLLAND *see under* DENIS DIDEROT

VOLTAIRE (1694–1778) *157*

Olympe Dunoyer and François Marie Arouet (he assumed the name Voltaire in 1718) did escape to Scheveningen, but they were soon caught and separated. Olympe was married off by her mother to a wealthy count. Arouet was sent to work in a lawyer's office in Paris.

Select Letters of Voltaire, edited by Theodore Besterman (Nelson, 1963)

Voltaire by J. E. N. Hearsey (Constable, 1976)

W

CONSTANZE WEBER (1763–1842) *see under* WOLFGANG AMADEUS MOZART

LAURENCE WHISTLER (1912–   ) *see under* JILL FURSE

CLARA WIECK (1819–1896) *see under* ROBERT SCHUMANN

OSCAR WILDE (1856–1900) *63*

In 1891 Oscar Wilde became infatuated with 'Bosie', Lord Alfred Douglas. Two years later Bosie's father, the Marquess of Queensberry, angered at a relationship he could not comprehend, sent Wilde a note calling him a 'sodomite'. Wilde sued the Marquess for criminal libel, but lost the case and became liable for prosecution. He was convicted, and spent two years in prison; on coming out he went abroad, and was joined by Bosie for some months.

The Letters of Oscar Wilde, edited by Rupert Hart-Davis (Granada, 1962; Harcourt, Brace & World, 1962)

Oscar Wilde by Philippe Jullian (Constable, 1969; Viking, 1969)

KING WILLIAM III (1650–1702)   *see under* QUEEN MARY II

ELIZABETH WILSON   *see under* WALTER BAGEHOT

MARY WOLLSTONECRAFT (1759–1797)   *181*

In the 1790s Mary met a handsome American, Gilbert Imlay, in Paris. For the first time in her life she was idyllically happy. But he soon began to tire of her and, after the birth of her daughter Fanny, disappeared to London. In despair, Mary twice tried to commit suicide. Though she later married the writer and philosopher William Godwin the elder, her deepest feelings were always for Imlay. Mary died giving birth to a daughter, Mary (who became the poet Shelley's second wife).

The Life and Death of Mary Wollstonecraft by Claire Tomalin (Weidenfeld, 1974; Harcourt Brace Jovanovich, 1975)

MARY ANNE WYNDHAM LEWIS   *see under* BENJAMIN DISRAELI

A NOTE ON THE TYPE

The text of this book was set in Apollo, the first typeface ever designed specifically for film composition.
Designed by Adrian Frutizer and issued by The Mono-
type Corporation of London in 1964, Apollo is not only
a versatile typeface suitable for many uses but also
pleasant to read in all of its sizes.

Composed by Keyspools Limited, Golborne, Lancashire, Great Britain,
and by Holmes Typography, Inc., San Jose, California

Printed and bound by The Haddon Craftsmen, Inc., Scranton, Pennsylvania

Illustrations by James Hutcheson